HOW TO WRITE NOVELS

Other Allison & Busby Writers' Guides:

HOW TO
WRITE CRIME
NOVELS
Isobel Lambot

ALLISON & BUSBY

First published in 1992 by
Allison & Busby
an imprint of Virgin Publishing Ltd
338 Ladbroke Grove
London W10 5AH
Copyright © Isobel Lambot 1992
ISBN 0 74900 125 9
A catalogue record for this title is available from the British Library
Phototypeset by Intype, London
Printed and bound in Great Britain by
Mackays of Chatham PLC, Chatham, Kent

CONTENTS

    The attractions of crime fiction. Types of crime fiction.
    *Whodunnits. Suspense. Psychological crime. Hard-
    boiled. Police procedural. Historical crime. Light-
    hearted/comedy thrillers. Action thrillers. Espionage.
    Off-beats.* The job of the crime writer. A debut in
    crime writing.

    First ideas. *Human relationships. Overheard conver-
    sations. Happenings in real life. Personal experiences.
    Past events. Out-of-place people or things. Places.
    Challenges. 'Finds'. Methods of murder. Alibis. The
    locked room.* From idea to plot. *Working up the idea.
    Motives. Establishing the theme.* Introducing the
    worked example. *Worked example – Death Trap I.*
    Exercise 1.

    Planning the crime. *The background. The events lead-
    ing up to the crime. The victim. The criminal. The
    motive.* What goes wrong. The investigation. Techni-
    cal aspects of the crime. *Ways and means of murder.
    Disposal of the body. Handling technical data.* Sources
    of information. *Police. Pathology. Forensic science.
    Other specialist information.* Developing the plot. *The
    involvement of the main characters. Other characters.*

FOREWORD

In over twenty years of crime writing, a period of running a creative writing class, lecturing to women's organisations, luncheon clubs, and writers' circles, I have always found a great interest in the way a crime novel is written. Each writer has an individual approach to the subject, so I do not feel that I am treading on the toes of others who have put down their thoughts on how this sort of writing should be done. Among such books currently in print are H. R. F. Keating's *Writing Crime Fiction*, Lisanne Radice's *The Way to Write Crime Fiction*, and Julian Symons's *Bloody Murder*. All of us have something to contribute out of our experience as writers and readers, but this does not necessarily mean that we all agree with each other; yet another book on the subject will give the would-be crime writer a different angle.

The aim of this handbook is that of practical teaching, using a worked example and proposing exercises for any reader who really wants to try their hand. Crime fiction is an umbrella category which covers a number of different, but related, sorts of story. The common factor is the crime element, and, largely, a shared readership. Inevitably, the teaching in this handbook is derived from my experience in the types of novel which I write: the detective and suspense story. However, I am convinced that the basic principles are the same for all types of crime writing.

All novels – of any sort, crime or 'straight' – are concerned with describing human behaviour in the context of the plot. Success or failure depend upon the credibility of both the characters and the action. For too long, crime fiction has been left on the side, as something not generally expected to be either well written or to have subject matter worthy of the term 'novel'. Fortunately, modern trends are moving against this prejudice. Crime writers should aim to produce work as well written and acceptable to the general reader as mainstream novels. I hope I have given some pointers as to how this may be done.

Isobel Lambot

ACKNOWLEDGEMENTS

The author wishes to express her gratitude to the following people for their invaluable assistance in the preparation of this handbook:

Mr John Kennedy Melling, FCA, FRSA, for help in compilation of the reading list.

Mr Peter Lovesey and Mr James Melville for information regarding their own work.

Mr Desmond Clay, for help over legal procedures.

Mrs Betty Hardwicke, for giving access to the work of the late Mr Glyn Hardwicke on legal matters.

Former Detective Superintendent Alan Poulton, and the West Mercia Constabulary, for help over police procedures.

Mr R. Williams, Editor of the *Mid-Wales Journal*, for permission to quote an inquest report.

Mr Ralph Spurrier, for providing books.

Professor Joan Rhys, MA, Ph.D., FRSL, for checking the typescript.

READING LIST

General

Murder Will Out	T. J. Binyon
Bedside Companion to Crime	H. R. F. Keating (ed.)
Crime Writers	H. R. F. Keating (ed.)
Murder Done to Death	John Kennedy Melling
The Mystery Writer's Art	Francis M. Nevins Jr (ed.)
An Introduction to the Detective Story	Leroy Lad Panek

Specialised

Fact and Fiction in Psychology	H. J. Eysenck
An Outline of Scientific Criminology	Nigel Morland
Murder, Suicide or Accident	Bernard Picton
The Expert	Bernard Picton
Book of Poisons	Gustav Shenk
Forensic Medicine	Simpson and Knight
Forty Years of Murder	Keith Simpson
Cause of Death	Frank Smyth (ed.)
Deadly Doses	Serita Deborah Stevens and Anne Klarner
Written in Blood	Colin Wilson

Criminal Evidence, Pleading & Practice	Archbold
Acting on Information Received (procedure from arrest to trial in novel form. Easy reading).	Glyn Hardwicke

Books every writer should possess:
Writers' & Artists' Yearbook
A good dictionary
Roget's Thesaurus
Fowler's Modern English Usage

1

INTRODUCTION TO CRIME WRITING

Crime writers need make no apologies for what they do. The fact that their craft is, at most, no more than two hundred years old does not make it inferior to other forms of novel-writing. Crime writers make a sizeable contribution towards meeting the demand of the reading public for entertainment literature. Specifically, they cater for the unfailing fascination that crime has for the law-abiding majority.

In the past, the public had to be satisfied with such things as the Newgate Calendar and broadsheets recording the last words of felons at the foot of the gallows. But this was real-life material, generally published for the moral improvement of the masses. It is questionable whether it made more than a surface impression on a populace which regarded attending a public execution as a good day out, and which made heroes of highwaymen.

The crudeness of all this was a reflection of the harsh conditions of the time, just as the popularity of folk heroes robbing the rich to give to the deserving poor, and the romanticising of cutthroats into daring adventurers flouting oppressive authority expressed innate social discontent.

The past two hundred years have brought profound changes in society as industrialisation has redistributed wealth and political power. The old order may have vanished, but crime still flourishes and public interest in it is undiminished. Daily newspapers record real-life crime, and occasionally a sensational trial catches the general imagination, but the diet of crime ingested by most readers is pure fiction. This is the great innovation which, from small beginnings in the early nineteenth century, has mushroomed into a lively industry. The history of the development of crime fiction is engrossing. In the Reading List are several excellent books on the subject.

The attractions of crime fiction

The entertainment value of crime fiction does not lie in an appeal to baser human instincts, or in taking pleasure in the misfortunes of others. Crime, as such, is an evil thing. People get hurt; crime is sordid; and, what is worse, in real life it often goes unpunished.

Essentially, crime fiction is concerned with justice, which may or may not be carried out by the legal authority. This appeals to the sense of justice in-built in most human beings, who would like to think that wrongs are righted, evil punished, and villains are given their just deserts.

It is no coincidence that the first stories which can properly be called crime fiction appeared at the time when modern police forces were being formed, and a new character, the 'detective' was created.

The idea of detection seized the imagination of the reading public. In the early stories, solutions were reached mainly by the power of pure reason, there being few or no scientific aids available to investigators. This had an intellectual appeal which has been the basis of mainstream crime writing ever since.

The fascination of the search for truth lies in a wide range of factors: from the thought processes of the detective who solves problems without moving from his chair, through the meticulous sifting of evidence by the forensic scientist, the high-powered policeman and all the dozens of fictional detectives, both private and amateur, to the tough guy walking the mean streets of the cities, fighting crime with its own weapons, and the smooth psychiatrist laying bare the roots of murder in a human heart. There is something for almost every reader within the body of work which presents itself as crime fiction.

Detective stories of one sort or another do not comprise the whole range. The genre also takes in thrillers, where the emphasis is on action rather than investigation, and spy stories, as well as fringe novels which can be described as 'off-beats'. Linking factors between these and mainstream crime stories are shared readership and, at times, shared authorship.

Types of crime fiction

It is impossible to fit different types of crime novels into separate and watertight compartments. The lines of demarcation between the detective story and the adventure story have never been clear, any more than those between detection by deduction and detection by the application of psychology. Yet some sort of categorisation has to be attempted for beginners to find their way.

Whodunnits

The word 'whodunnit' implies a plot based on a puzzle. This is the classic 'straight' detective story. The progression is as follows: a crime, the investigation, the unveiling of the murderer at the end. Clues are planted throughout the book for the use of both detective and reader. In the 1930s, the so-called Golden Age of the whodunnit, it was the favourite territory of the gifted amateur and private professional detectives such as Lord Peter Wimsey, Albert Campion, Hercule Poirot and Nero Wolfe, to name a few.

The plot is not as rigid as it sounds, and has been subjected to many variations. It can be inverted, with the murderer revealed to the reader at the start, while the detective knows nothing; here the reader's interest is held by the skill of the hunt. Alternatively, neither murderer nor detective is identified until the moment of truth at the end.

It is true that fewer 'classical' whodunnits are written nowadays, and critics regard the form to be in decline or extinct. This dismissal deserves examination in the face of the only statistics available: sales. Inevitably, this leads to the prime exponent of the whodunnit, Agatha Christie, whose sales are still phenomenal and worldwide. Adverse criticism of her work is endless, but the reading public expresses its preference in no uncertain manner. There must be lessons to learn from this. My own view is that while the gifted amateur is no longer a credible detective in these days of advanced forensic science, the old formula of puzzle-and-red-herrings has not lost its appeal.

Modern examples: Robert Barnard: *Death in Purple Prose*, Lisa Cody: *Backhand*; Michael Z. Lewin: *Called by a Panther*.

Suspense

The suspense novel depends upon mystification and ever-looming menace and danger to the character upon whom the plot hinges. The crime element may be murder, blackmail, robbery, kidnapping, terrorism, or any other sort of mayhem. The unravelling of the mystery may be by straightforward detection, but the puzzle element will be played down, and successive suspects are not set up as red herrings. The solution is often brought about by dramatic action, with the main character placed in mortal peril, rather than by a reasoned exposure of a criminal.

This is one end of the range covered by the suspense novel, where the borderline between whodunnits and suspense is blurred, and both sorts of book are written by the same authors. At the other end of the range are novels of a more romantic nature, the descendants of the gothic novels of the eighteenth and nineteenth centuries. Here the main character is denied the support of professional detectives, and will be obliged to blunder through a series of dreadful experiences until s/he finds herself/himself face to face with the enemy. Usually there is a strong love interest to complicate the issue.

The suspense novel commands a large readership. Everyone likes to experience the occasional shiver down the spine. From a writer's point of view, the concentration of the action upon one character invites the reader to identify with that character; once that is accomplished, the reader will want to continue reading and find out what happens to that character. From the point of view of a beginner, unless one is strongly drawn to one of the other types of crime novel, the suspense novel is a good starting point.

Examples: Paula Gosling: *The Brass Monkey*; Marian Babson: *Past Regrets*.

Psychological crime

A distinction has to be drawn between novels about psychologists who detect, and novels about the progress of a crime through the complex of emotions which motivate it.

Psychologist detectives may be professionals, such as Gladys Mitchell's Mrs Lestrange Bradley, or, in contemporary writing, Jonathan Kellerman's Dr Alex Delaware. Alternatively, they may be people who would not describe themselves as psychologists, who have no qualifications other than a deep knowledge of human behaviour. The best examples are two of the most famous fictional detectives: Chesterton's Father Brown, and Agatha Christie's Miss Marple.

The other type of psychological crime novel is not about whodunnit, but whydunnit. This comes in different forms. It may involve the building up of pressures on the main character until the explosion into murder; the discovery the identity of a killer through exposing the emotions of the victim's immediate circle; or the problem of the random attacker, the psychopath – the person who, though apparently normal, kills strangers or little children.

Examples: Ruth Rendell: *The Bridesmaid*; Jonathan Kellerman: *Butcher's Theatre*; Eileen Dewhurst: *A Private Prosecution*; Anthea Fraser: *The April Rainers*.

Hard-boiled

The unforeseen results of introducing Prohibition into America – bootlegging, gangsters, gang shoot-ups, police corruption – also brought to the fore a new style of crime writing. This was the tough, terse narration of the activities of the 'private eye'. It was an attempt to bring realism to crime fiction. The settings are genuine enough: the mean streets of the big cities, where every imaginable form of crime and vice is to be found. So are the criminals, the gangs who control and profit from the crime and vice. What is purely fictional is the character of the private eye himself, the transference of the gunslinger of the lawless Wild West to the now equally lawless city. He is a man who works alone and deals out his own code of justice.

Stylised or not, the hard-boiled detective is an enduring character with a big following. The fascination is in the furious pace of the action and the staccato narration. Violence is built in, native to the setting. These stories depend upon a tight plot and a collection of smart villains and double-crossing dames. Endings are often wry, and match the cynicism of the private eye.

Modern examples: Russell James: *Payback*; Sue Grafton: *A Is for Alibi*.

Police procedural

For a long time, most fictional policemen were portrayed as thick-headed plods only too happy to defer to the brilliant amateur who solved their cases for them. This misrepresentation has been corrected by the rise of the police novel. A modern murder investigation is a complex and fascinating affair. The techniques are a fascinating mixture of old and new; the resources of a highly skilled team of experts backed by the forensic laboratory are combined with the work of constables in the hard grind of fingertip searches.

The police novel falls into two broad categories: the single detective with his immediate assistants; and the operation of a department, with several detectives investigating whatever crimes turn up.

The first category is very much in the English tradition, with concentration on the crime in hand. The second originated in America, and is an attempt at realism, to show police work in its drudgery as well as its triumphs. A group of detectives – a unit, a squad, a shift – is followed over a period of days, illustrating not only the work but also the private lives of the detectives and their families. Technically it is difficult to knit this sort of narrative into an acceptable whole, with a beginning and an end. These novels are usually designed as series, building up a readership through interest in the detectives as people, and this in itself holds the danger that the continued histories of the group may evolve into a soap opera about their families, their hang-ups, their problems, with crime providing little more than a backdrop.

Examples: James Melville: *The Bogus Buddha* (single

detective); Ed McBain: *Sadie When She Died* (87th Precinct group)

Historical crime

The popularity of historical detective stories is comparatively new. In the past, there have been sporadic examples, such as Melville Davisson Post's Uncle Abner stories, and Robert Van Gulik's novels about Judge Dee, set in medieval China.

Modern writers, generally, prefer Victorian England as a setting. There are obvious advantages: the period is well documented; it is not so far removed from our own age as to require explanations of an alien culture, although manners and social habits were different; and police forces existed.

Yet the detective who has swept the board belongs way back in the twelfth century – Ellis Peters's Brother Cadfael. These novels are beautifully constructed and clearly meticulously researched. Cadfael himself is fictitious, but he has been put into the real setting of the Benedictine Abbey of Shrewsbury.

The success of these stories has inevitably brought a crowd of imitators. Beginners are not advised to jump on such bandwagons. An imitator has to be superlatively good to overtake the original.

Peter Lovesey, who has written some excellent stories featuring the Victorian Sergeant Cribb, also has attempted to use a real-life historical figure as detective. This is not breaking new ground. Lillian de la Torre wrote short stories about Dr Johnson's investigations into crime – narrated, naturally, by Boswell.

Another new field has been opened up by television adaptations of Sayers, Allingham and Christie, which treat the stories as period pieces. There is a lot of scope, as well as interesting backgrounds, in the 1920s and 30s, and research material is abundant.

Examples: Ellis Peters: *The Potter's Field*; Peter Lovesey: *Bertie and the Tinman.*

Light-hearted/comedy thrillers

The light-hearted detective story is a serious crime story treated lightly, with wit and humour, and written in a style which fizzes along. The essence of black comedy is that the characters act in all seriousness. The combination of their own human failings and bizarre situations provides the fun. The pace of the action needs to be hot.

The comic detective story takes the light-hearted crime novel well over the threshold of probability. Many are pastiches of famous fictional detectives, Sherlock Holmes being the favourite victim.

There is no reason why a light-hearted thriller should not be used for a crime-writing debut, but it would be advisable to limit the lightness to the style rather than the content. A word of warning: comedy can be difficult to sell.

Examples: Miles Franklin: *Bring the Monkey* (old spoof, reprinted); Simon Brett: *A Nice Class of Corpse*.

Action thrillers

The action thriller is distinguished from the adventure yarn by the presence of the crime element. This is a large market, reaching people who would never pick up a detective story. A glance at the work of Alastair MacLean, Dick Francis, and Desmond Bagley reveals that half the appeal is the specialist knowledge about the background. A good plot alone will not carry the story.

Detailed knowledge is needed in all sorts of fields: weaponry, ships, aircraft, radio communications, survival techniques, industrial processes and so on. The excellence of this sort of inside information contributes enormously to the success of the book. Settings, too, have to be detailed, with the physical location of the story an integral part of the plot.

Suspense elements over and above the physical demands of the plot are essential. Emotional tensions will arise in any group of people under strain, especially when there is some sort of criminal activity in progress. The reader may know who is doing what, so that the suspense lies in how they can be stopped or caught; or there may be a hidden traitor in the ranks who will be unveiled at the end.

Intensive research has to be carried out before tackling an action thriller. Writers who are engineers, physicists, professional soldiers or ex-jockeys have the edge over the rest of us.

Examples: Dick Francis: *Straight*; Craig Thomas: *The Last Raven*.

Espionage

The spy story has become a sub-genre of the crime novel because the activities of secret agents are against the law. A foreign spy, if caught, is tried and sent to prison; a national, subverted by money or through ideological conviction, is arraigned for treason, for which the death penalty still applies, in theory at any rate. The police are involved through Special Branch.

The crimes of murder, blackmail, and kidnapping are found in abundance in the dark world of espionage; the people who commit these crimes are hunted by detectives.

The political situation during most of the twentieth century has presented immense opportunities to the writers of spy stories. Spying is nothing new; what is remarkable in our time is the escalation of the activity.

The unexpected political upheaval of the sudden events of late 1989 has knocked the bottom out of spy stories for the moment. Until the political regrouping has settled, writers will have to make do with the remaining ideological enemies. In any case, the readership will still be there. Spy stories are exciting, and it will be a long time before the memory of the division of Europe will fade.

Examples: Len Deighton: *Spy Hook, Line, Sinker*; Gavin Lyall: *Uncle Target*.

Off-beats

It is difficult to describe an off-beat, precisely because it is unlike anything else. Highly original, they lie between crime and straight novels. They are *different*, which is something of a dirty word to agents and publishers. Writers write them to please themselves. The problem is selling them. An off-beat novel needs a devoted agent with the tenacity of a bulldog: such rare treasures may, on occasions, be found.

Fun as it is to write an off-beat, they are not recommended for a crime-writing debut.

Examples: Jessica Mann: *A Healthy Kind of Grave*; Alan Plater: *The Beiderbecke Tapes*.

The job of the crime writer

It is not the job of the crime writer to discuss the social implications of crime, but this is an error into which some critics of the genre fall. The crime writer's job is to accept the situation as it is, and from human situations – fuelled by pride, greed, lust, hatred, jealousy, fanaticism, madness and sheer badness – to create an interesting and ingenious plot.

The reader is held by the progress of the crime; the twists and turns; the impact upon the lives of the characters involved; and the way in which human unpredictability can ruin the cleverest of schemes; all culminating in a satisfactory ending.

This is far from the situations in real life, which are rarely cut and dried. Generally, crime writers observe certain conventions to round off the story:

- In a 'straight' detective story, the guilty party should be caught, or, at the very least, deprived of the profits of the crime.
- Where the hero is a Robin Hood figure, the crimes are against evildoers beyond the reach of the law, and the motive is to help the helpless so that the crimes are justified. In no way may the hero be caught.
- Raffles-type attractive villains, who keep the proceeds of their crimes, are acceptable, and appeal to our latent desires to see authority flouted.
- Master crooks and would-be Dominators of the World have to be foiled every time – but allowed to escape to reappear in future stories. The public loves a villain, and a larger-than-life one can lead to a profitable series.

22

These conventions work in the writer's own interest, since a satisfied reader will be willing to read more of the author's work. On the other hand, they underline the separation of fiction from fact. The crime writer is in the business of entertaining the reader, giving him the relaxation of a 'good read' after the day's work. There is no entertainment value attached to a mugging in an alley, common though it is in real life; yet the exploits of a greedy person systematically murdering the half a dozen relations standing between him and the family fortune can enthrall. Inevitably, the crime writer's material has to be of a sort which will expand into an interesting plot.

While accepting that the crimes we write about may not be very likely to occur in real life, we have to create an impression of reality so that the reader is persuaded that such an event *might* happen. This is done through the credibility of the characters, the believable background to the crime, and accuracy of technical details. The crime novel must relate to the readers' own experience of human behaviour and their knowledge of the world about them.

A debut in crime writing

The first choice facing a budding crime writer is that of deciding which type of story to write. Everyone must follow their own inclinations and tastes in crime fiction, and select the type in which they will feel most comfortable. Later, excursions can be made into other types; most writers take advantage of the blurred demarcation lines between, for example, the whodunnit and the suspense novel, and write in both categories. Straying into the hard-boiled when the writer is known for historical detective stories might try the patience of readers too far, and therefore a pseudonym should be used. However, all that is in the future. At the moment you need to select the type of crime story for your debut.

The second choice you must make is that of a detective, since most crime stories are concerned with some sort of investigation. This character can be:

- A professional, either police or private
- A professional from another discipline, e.g. a forensic scientist or a psychologist
- An amateur, with gifts of reasoning and/or intuition
- Someone who through force of circumstances is obliged to make their own search for the truth

Much will depend on the nature of the plot, but right from the start it is as well to have a clear idea of the character who will solve the mystery. The detective may or may not be the main character, but is bound to be important.

The choice between the various types of detective is personal, but should not strain the reader's credulity. The heyday of the gifted amateur would appear to be over: modern police officers are most unlikely to be willing to share their investigations with a latter-day Peter Wimsey, or to call in a Poirot. The private detective, amateur or professional, has most freedom to function in areas where the police are not investigating.

The vast majority of fictional detectives have been men, but over the years, there has been a good sprinkling of women, young and pretty or grandmotherly and apparently harmless. The modern trend is to portray women detectives doing a normal job of work, and being as tough as any man. Good examples are Lisa Cody's Anna Lee (private detective); and Susan Moody's Penny Wanawake (amateur).

In choosing a detective, the writer should have an eye to the future, and consider the possibility of featuring the character in a succession of books. A lot depends on the type of plot, which may dictate whether or not the end of the first book is the end of the road for its characters.

The whole point of writing a series featuring the same character is to create a continuing demand. Series characters have to be strongly individualistic, and can be on either side of the law. The problem is that writers can become slaves to their own creations; breaking free is not easy, as Conan Doyle discovered when he thought he had disposed of Sherlock Holmes over the Reichenbach Falls.

It is undeniable that the reading public likes series, so if a character's career seems worth pursuing, you should have an attempt at a second book. If it is not well received by agent/publisher, be brave enough to abandon it and stick to one-offs.

The third choice to be made is whether or not to include a love interest. Here, again, it is a matter of personal choice and the dictates of the plot. In my own view, readers in general like a love interest, as long as it is relevant to the plot, and in my earlier work one was included. However, I am now less likely to regard a love interest as an essential, though I do not rule it out. Among crime writers, there is a great division of opinion over love interests.

Once you have made these choices, you will then need to start on the construction of a plot. To make the process of writing a crime novel clear, a worked example is used as illustration in Chapters 2 to 7, and the reader is invited to do a practical exercise.

2

IDEAS AND THEME

Novels have small beginnings. Plots do not leap to the mind fully formed. What is needed to trigger the imagination is an idea which promises a story if investigated.

The process is entirely subjective: what appeals to one person leaves another cold. This is the problem when people offer ideas – 'Here's something to put in one of your books.' It is *their* imagination which has been fired, and if the telling of the tale does not raise a similar spark in the author, the idea cannot be used.

The unexpected spark of a first idea often comes at an awkward moment, when one is in no position to do anything much about it. The idea can vanish as quickly as it comes, so it is advisable to jot down enough to fix the idea in the memory.

First ideas

There are many sources from which ideas spring, and most come to the author during the course of everyday life. By this, I do not mean that crime writers are in the habit of falling over corpses, but rather that their creative imagination transforms the ordinary into the exciting.

Here are some common sources of first ideas for crime novels:

Human relationships

People have to live with one another, and this causes stress in any family, neighbourhood or community. Different ways of living, behaviour, work and leisure cause friction. Shared blood does not promise shared characters, ambitions, likes or dislikes; neither does it promise happy and normal relationships between parents and children, or between siblings and other members of the family group.

Choice of friends brings conflict in families as the ideas of different generations clash. Fierce quarrels with neighbours break out over trivialities: disputes over boundary fences, overhanging trees, noisy children and pets. This sort of friction occurs, also, at the workplace, in the local pub, in sports teams and golf clubs, and among church congregations.

People have an ingrained habit of falling out with each other. Quarrels may look like storms in a teacup, but for those involved, the results can range from petty nastinesses to the ultimate crime of murder.

Overheard conversations

Blatant eavesdropping is an author's habit. Snatches of conversation, caught out of context in the street, in a bus or a restaurant, can set the imagination alight. Everyone's favourite topics of conversation are, in order, themselves, and other people – more often than not, their opinions of others is a critical one. A simple phrase such as 'Tell him I'm waiting' or 'It won't happen again, I'll see to that' calls up endless possibilities.

Happenings in real life

Newspaper reports are a useful source, but what is reported is most likely to be some sordid crime, quickly solved and not the material for a novel. Transformed by the imagination, however, the report will become the invisible peg for a fictional crime which will not be solved before the final chapter.

27

It is advisable to cut out snippets which catch your interest in the daily papers. You never know when you might want to make use of them.

Personal experiences

Some 'straight' novelists spend their working days writing up their own experiences in one way or another, in book after book. Whenever I am asked if I do this, my reply is to point out that I write about murder.

Even if suitable, the use of autobiographical material in a crime novel is undesirable – fact will always interfere with the creative process – but there is no reason why situations in which either the author or personal friends have found themselves should not be used. What must be discarded is the development of the situation in real life – in other words, what actually happened; it is only the situation itself which sparks off the fictional plot.

The *situation* might be recognisable – friends may or may not be flattered by its use – but the characters themselves should not resemble those actually involved, or, once again, flexibility will be lost and the creative imagination restricted.

This sort of first idea should be treated in the same way as one arising from a newspaper report.

Past events

There is something compelling about the past – one's own and other people's – which is much heightened when a piece of it breaks through into the present. None of us can escape the influence of the past: it is what has brought us to our present state, and its long shadow reaches into the future. It is a wonderful gift to the novelist.

Out-of-place people or things

These are first-class sources of ideas. The sight of something totally incongruous cannot help but fire the imagination. It is the excitement of the unexpected, the inexplicable, the illogical that makes questions leap to mind.

Places

Landscapes, woods, rivers, gardens, and, above all, houses appeal to more than just the eyes. Atmosphere pervades them: a shiver can run down the spine on first perceiving 'a lovely place for a murder'. The sinister-looking house has been used time and again in murder novels, and it will go on being used.

A place of great beauty – a lovely building, an enchanting garden – can also present an interesting setting for crime, contrasting the attractiveness of the place with the unpleasantness of human behaviour.

Challenges

A challenge is a demand to the creative mind to perform, not when it is stimulated, but to order.

Short-story competitions sometimes present an opening paragraph to be continued by entrants, or provide a ready-made cast of characters. This is a manufactured stimulus, like prodding a sleeping animal. The astonishing thing is that it works. It is amazing how quickly the mind will respond, even if one is not interested in the competition.

'Finds'

These range from the map of buried treasure in the adventure stories of our childhood to the well-worn idea of discovering something in an antique shop, or buying an old house and coming across something peculiar walled up in it. This latter variation took on a whole new meaning to crime writers after the grisly discoveries in the house and garden at 10 Rillington Place.

There is no denying that these 'finds' happen. The difficulty is making a satisfactory novel out of them. The actuality hampers the imagination and, in some cases, there is the possibility that living people may be hurt or enraged. No author wishes to be run out of a nice peaceful English village. The only solution is to take the 'find' out of its real context and invent another for it.

Methods of murder

Thinking about ways of killing people is a crime writer's business. It is perfectly possible to come up with a new and original way of doing it perhaps with the use of an unusual weapon, or the devising of a clever trap.

Alibis

Here the means of murder may be mundane; it is the way of escaping suspicion which has come first to the author's mind.

The locked room

Consider the complicated puzzle of the locked room: there is a dead body inside, no question of suicide, no weapon, no apparent means of escape for the murderer. The solving of the problem of the room is the whole point of the novel. Once the problem is solved, the murderer is found.

The locked room has a long history in crime fiction. Advances in technology must have provided fresh opportunities for locked room mysteries.

First ideas from these last three sources are purely intellectual and are not sufficient in themselves to make a crime novel. If they are to blossom into novels, the human element has to be injected. Murders, alibis and locked room puzzles all need human hands to set the ball rolling.

From idea to plot

Being struck by an idea is an exciting event. The imagination starts rushing off in several directions, mostly up blind alleys. The temptation is to plunge immediately into the creation of a plot. All too often, the whole process will suddenly come to a stop. This is because there is a definite sequence to building a novel out of a first idea.

The sequence is:

1 the first idea strikes
2 working up the idea
3 establishing the theme
4 building the plot.

Working up the idea

This is an exercise in disciplining the imagination, letting it chew at the idea, writing down all the various secondary ideas which spring from it, then sorting them out into which to keep and which to discard.

The idea has to be analysed, the points of importance extracted, to see what developments are possible.

Here are two examples to show how this might be done.

EXAMPLE 1. First idea: from a report of an inquest in the *Mid-Wales Journal* of 28 September 1990.

An open verdict was recorded at a Builth Wells inquest this week on a 41-year-old hill walker whose remains were discovered in one of the remotest parts of Britain last April.

Near the body of bachelor Graham Nuttall was his collie Ruswarp, so weak it could not stand. The RSPCA later recognised the dog's exceptional bravery and devotion in guarding its master's body.

Mr Nuttall lived alone at Burnley, Lancashire, with Ruswarp. A railway enthusiast, he was described by neighbour Harry Sharples as a loner in good health.

Professor Bernard Knight, who carried out a post mortem examination on April 9, told Monday's inquest the body was badly decomposed, with no possibility of facial recognition.

There was no sign of physical violence and no cause of death could be offered.

A man in walking boots and an anorak answering to Mr Nuttall's description was seen on January 20 by Irving Murray, an electrical contractor working in the Elan Valley. He noticed the man's Burnley accent and that he had a black and white collie dog.

Mr Nuttall's body was discovered on April 7 at the Devil's Staircase, Abergwesyn, by another walker, David Clarke from Andover, Hampshire.

He told Alfons Van Hees, acting deputy coroner for south Powys, of spotting what appeared to be a ball of fluff. It turned out to be a dog which looked as though it was dead.

Mr Clarke said there was a pair of boots by the dog, which was half-starved and very weak. Then he came across a body in the River Irfon.

Constable Michael Richards said the body was wedged against a rock. Upstream on a bank were a pair of brown walking boots and the collie, which could not stand.

Detective-constable Howard Jones told of a search, which produced a rucksack in a wooded area. Inside was an envelope with Mr Nuttall's address on it.

There was no clue why clothing was further away from the body, said DC Jones.

He told Mr Van Hees inquiries were carried out and Mr Nuttall's death was not linked to any other incident. There were no inquiries at present.

Recording the open verdict, the coroner said no precise date could be given for the death of Mr Nuttall. whose body was ravaged by animals.

There were no discernible signs of injury, but the cause of death was unascertainable. There was no evidence to show whether or not death was due to natural causes or an accident.

Analysis

- The victim was last seen alive on 20 January.
- The body was found on 7 April.
- The pathologist's evidence: no cause of death offered; the body was badly decomposed, with no possibility of facial recognition; there was no way of determining the date of death.
- Curious facts: the body was wedged against a rock in the river; upstream was a pair of boots guarded by a starving dog; a rucksack containing an envelope with the name and address of a missing person was found in a wooded area; the police witness stated there was no clue as to why clothing was at a distance from the body.

Possible developments:

- The lone walker stumbled across something no one was supposed to see and was killed to shut his mouth.
- Discard the hints as to the personality of the dead man. Make him into someone different: have him on his way to a secret rendezvous, and killed either by the person he was to meet or waylaid by opponents. The scatter of clothing could suggest a fight or an attempt to escape.
- Discard the evidence of the dog, and there is no real evidence that the body was that of the missing person. Could that man have wanted to disappear, and chosen to murder someone to provide a body?

This example is a simple one, the newspaper report providing a lot of material. The second example is less concrete.

EXAMPLE 2. First idea: A human tangle – a dominating mother with two daughters, one much older than the other; the elder daughter has had her life lived for her by the mother; the younger has escaped and married (with the whole-hearted support of her sister, who does not wish to see her caught in the same trap from which she could not escape) a man of whom the mother disapproves; within a year, the mother has accepted the son-in-law and never ceases to sing his praises. The elder daughter, whose every suitor was turned away, cannot stomach this; resentment, bitterness and rage possess her.

Analysis

- Difference in character between the sisters. The younger is the stronger, stands up to her mother and comes out on top.
- The elder sister blames everyone else, not her own weakness, for her unhappy situation.
- The new son-in-law makes himself agreeable to the mother and wins her over.
- The mother turns defeat into triumph by ignoring her original opposition, and going on as if she had chosen this man for her daughter.

Possible developments

- The elder sister's resentment of supposed injustice to herself could boil over to the point of murdering her mother.
- Add a large inheritance in the hands of the mother, and the elder daughter could foresee her own share being either diminished or lost.
- The son-in-law may be a fortune-hunter; all the women may be at risk.

Motives

From the examination of these two examples, it is clear that any situation can produce a number of ideas for plots, all based on reactions to the problems inherent in it. From these ideas, you should pick out those which give the strongest motivation for the commission of a crime.

Motives spring from the weaknessess of human nature. At the top of the list are: greed; jealousy and envy; anger; sexual desire; hatred; revenge; fear of exposure; and pride of self, family, place.

To these may be added: lack of confidence in the efficacy of legal processes (leading the character to take the law into his own hands); lack of confidence in policing (leading to vigilante activities); obsessions; fanaticism; misplaced patriotism.

The difference between these two lists is that the first

covers motives which can be found anywhere, at any time, in any society, and in any person. For the second list, the field is narrower; fewer people would commit crimes for these reasons, and fewer sorts of crimes result from these motives.

Inevitably, the question of insanity, or diminished responsibility, arises. Without a doubt, psychopaths and sex maniacs are mentally abnormal, and courts have occasionally accepted pleas of diminished responsibility in other cases; but most crimes against other people are deliberately committed.

The lesson to be drawn from this by the beginner in crime writing is to make sure that the motive is strong enough to give credibility to the plot. Crime, even fictional crime, is a serious business.

In many crime novels, the uncovering of the motive reveals the criminal. In these cases, readers will guess accurately the identity of this character as soon as a smell of the motive appears. On the other hand, readers will feel cheated if the motive is jumped on them without previous preparation. To avoid falling between these two stools, other reasonable motives need to extracted from the plot and its characters so that suspicion can move in different directions.

Establishing the theme

It is this combination of first idea and its development with the motives which can arise from it which produces the underlying theme of the novel.

The theme is the backbone of the work, the thread running through it and giving it coherence. It is important to distinguish between the theme of the novel and its plot. The theme is what the novel is about; the plot is how the theme is presented through the characters and the action.

The essence of the theme is conflict – the problem which has to be worked out by the end of the novel. The conflict comes in clashes of personalities or ambitions, divided loyalties, loves and hates. The problems are as diverse as the messes human beings get themselves into.

In selecting themes, crime writers use resources common to all types of novel. Human situations can develop in any direction the novelist pleases. Some specific event must initiate the action which will demonstrate the working-out of the theme. For crime writers this event is the crime itself – the circumstances from which it arises, its commission, or the aftermath, according to the type of story.

Crimes, once committed, produce violent changes in the lives of those involved, changes from which no one is likely to recover fully. Crimes are catalysts which bring people face to face with themselves – an unpleasant experience which can turn out to be catastrophic. Polite veneers do not stand up to the impact of crime, nor do many estimates of self-importance. The crime writer exploits the human situations which engender crime and the human reactions to it, and no matter how clever the plot, it is the human interest which holds the reader's attention.

The actual choice of theme is highly individual. First ideas can lead to many different themes, but the one selected is that which appeals to the author's own particular interests at the time of writing. It is impossible to write convincingly about a theme unless one has something special to say about it.

All novels make statements of one sort or another. Some are written for purposes of propaganda, and the grinding of ideological axes. With crime novels, this is not generally the case, nor, in my view, should it be. Primarily, our job is to entertain, to relax the mind, to add an exotic touch to the humdrum round. Yet crime writers cannot escape from the obligation of feeling intensely about their themes, whether it is an intimate family problem or the intrusion into ordinary lives of terrorists, psychopaths or rapists.

Themes can be summed up briefly, in one or two words. Themes from the examples of first ideas, cited above, could be as follows.

Example 1: fear of exposure (the chance, unwanted witness); violence for a cause (the savage underworld of the terrorist, spy etc); freedom (the desire to cut all ties).

Example 2: revenge (for past injuries, imagined or otherwise); justice (safeguarding the proper share of the inheritance); greed (to gather everything into the son-in-law's hands).

One of the commonest themes is self-development. Plots involving situations of terror, traps, miscarriages of justice, dangerous enterprises and so on, give their characters a rough ride. Survival depends upon the development of strengths and overcoming weaknesses. Fear, in any form, is a great educator. So is shared experience, which forms life-long links among survivors.

Introducing the worked example

This worked example is taken from a suspense story, entitled *Death Trap*, which I wrote some years ago. It was bought by D.C. Thompson & Co., Ltd., as a serial for one of their newspapers. Later, it was serialised in Sweden. Since it is a real plot, there are faults in it. I have resisted the temptation to correct these. I invite readers to look for them; it will be good practice for criticising their own work.

Worked example – Death Trap I

First idea: this was drawn from the situation of a woman friend who moved to another town and into a close-knit group of neighbours. One of these was an older man who showed signs of interest in her but failed to follow them up in a recognisable fashion. This came as something of a surprise to an attractive and intelligent young woman.

Analysis

- The girl is alone and has to find her feet among strangers.
- What situation has she walked into? What cross-currents link this group?
- Why does the male neighbour behave as he does? Is he moving towards her in an original fashion? Or is he running away? Or what else?
- Is the girl sufficiently intrigued to want to know more about him? Or does she find him a nuisance and an obstacle to settling down in her new environment?

This first idea gives a human situation – that of a stranger pitched into a closed society – but no hint of what might turn this situation into a theme for a crime novel.

Secondary idea is needed. The two previous tenants of her new home have died in suspicious circumstances.

Analysis

- The inference is that the crimes have not been cleared up.
- Is the girl some sort of investigator?
- Or is she ignorant of the deaths, and has taken the place by chance, or by the contrivance of some other party? Is this the source of the man's interest in her? Who has sent her, blind, into a trap?

I chose the second possibility, because the idea of an innocent person caught in a trap appeals to me, and raises the question of what that person can do about it.

Self-development then, is the theme as the girl tries to find out what she has got into, who got her there, and how she might extricate herself.

Exercise 1

Here are some first ideas. Analyse each to bring out the points which strike you. Then see what themes you can make from them.

1. The peculiar relationship between identical twins: similarities in appearance; telepathic sympathy in knowing when the other is hurt or in trouble; dissimilarities in character and fingerprints.
2. A *This is Your Life*-type programme. The subject is an elderly man, now famous. An old acquaintance bounds on to the stage, full of joviality. The subject promptly punches him on the nose, declaring that he has been waiting for an opportunity to do that for forty years.
3. A man with clothes covered with blood is seen on a bus. No one takes any notice. Only hours afterwards do the conductor and some passengers connect him with a police-hunt for a violent murderer. (This was a real-life incident.)

38

3

THE CRIME

The theme now established, we can begin to think about building the plot. Be prepared for a good many false starts. Ideas come freely once one starts thinking about a plot. Make notes on every good idea which presents itself. Out of them all, you will make a good plot. Be flexible, and discard ideas which do not appear to work, even if those ideas are your favourites.

The crime is the focal point of the action. Whether it comes at the beginning, the middle or the end of the novel this still holds true. When it comes early on, or before the point where the novel opens, the actions of all the characters are under its direct influence. If the first part of the book is working up to the crime, only the actions of those characters directly involved will be governed by it. The others are in ignorance of what is about to happen; only once the crime is committed will their actions be conditioned by it. Only in the case of the psychological novel, where pressures are built up to explode into a crime at the end, will most of the characters be unaware of the danger until the moment of shock at the end.

Planning the crime

Plotting begins with the crime: its background, the events leading up to it, the victim, the criminal, the motive and, most important in all plots involving detection, what goes wrong with it: that is, why the perpetrator, who imagines he has covered his tracks, should ever be caught.

The background

Generally, it is inadvisable to open the first chapter with the origins of the crime. These roots may reach far back into the past of the characters, but for the reader to be aware of them may remove all suspense from the action. Yet, the information has to be put across so that the logic of the crime is understood. Conan Doyle was well aware of the problem of how this is to be done when he was writing *The Valley of Fear*. His solution was to include at the end a long section, amounting to a novelette, explaining the origin of the crime, a deadly device which should be held up as a warning to crime writers. Knowing the outcome, most modern readers would find it boring.

In most crime novels, the causes of the crime are revealed piecemeal, as the evidence builds up. To give the situation a gloss of credibility, and to build up the right sort of psychological make-up for the criminal, the author needs to work out, in advance, every detail of how the situation in which the crime is committed comes about.

The events leading up to the crime

Most crime stories involving detection build up to the crime so that the victim is seen in action amongst the other characters. This gives an opportunity for the planting of clues in advance of the crime, and for throwing suspicion on other characters, who may later be used as red herrings.

Where the book opens with the finding of a corpse, the detective has to dig into the preceding events at once, and looks for alibis to eliminate as many as possible of his suspects.

In planning the countdown to a murder, it is often helpful to make a chart of the movements of all the characters.

EXAMPLE: A man is killed when he goes to his garage to take out his car. He has entered by a side door, put on the light, and opened the double door from the inside. From the position of the body, it appears that he has been attacked from behind as he was about to unlock the driver's door. There are four people who had reason to kill him. Vital times are 10.30 to 12.30

THE CRIME

Time	Characters			
	1	2	3	4
10.30a.m.	Alone in house	In shop	On train	In wait at side of garage
11.30a.m.	Alone in house	on bus	On train	Kills, victim, drives to next station up line, boards train
12.30p.m.	Finds body	At home	Leaves train meets 4 and assumes that 4 has been on train all the way	Leaves train Fools 3

The chart shows that Character 1 has no alibi and is the one to find the body (always suspicious); 2's alibi depends on witnesses (shop assistant, bus conductor) who may not remember him; 3 has an alibi (booking clerk, other passengers known to him); Character 4 knows 3 will be on train, and uses him to back up own (false) alibi.

The chart helps the writer to keep tabs on the characters at the vital times, and makes plotting an intricate sequence of events easier.

The victim

Where a murder is committed before the book opens, or the body is discovered on the first page, the impact of the personality of the victim is not lessened. The shadow of the victim spreads over all the action, as the investigation proceeds.

Victims move within their own social groups: home, family, workplace, leisure activities. Some event within one of these groups has caused the murder – this can also hold true where victims are chosen at random. People who are attacked on commuter trains, or when they get off them, are travelling within their work patterns. Children who are abducted are grabbed from their habitual places of play.

The criminal

In most crime novels, the criminal is found within one of the social groups which also contain the murderee. This character has to be selected carefully. It is inadvisable to make the most unpleasant character the murderer; the reader will latch on to such a person as the front runner very quickly. On the contrary, the best crime novels often show a certain sympathy for the villain, and it is a truism to say that no one is all bad.

Only psychopaths are 'born murderers', and that trait is generally seen early in life. This does not make them any less dangerous, especially where there has been a family cover-up for the sake of respectability.

Ordinary people can be driven to murder, given sufficient pressure with no hope of release, and most of us could lash out in sudden anger, using the nearest weapon to hand; but it takes a special sort of person to plan a murder in cold blood.

The motive

A wild slash with a poker, when driven beyond endurance, is uncomplicated and probably regretted as soon as done, but an act of deliberate murder requires an adequate motive.

The victims of most detective stories are people who stand in the way of others: the rich and mean aged relation; the unwanted wife; the colleague whose position is coveted; the unexpected witness; the one who knows too much. Such murders are planned. The one characteristic which stands out in relation to their killers is an abnormal love of self. Only the supreme egotist will go to the length of killing to remove someone from their path. No matter how much the murderers cover up their intentions, this characteristic of intense self-love cannot fail to have been observed by their family and friends.

Obsessions and fanaticism can distort a normal person, and there is no reason why even those closest to the murderer should realise the lengths to which they will go. One truly frightening aspect of modern society is the thought that the nice person next door might be making bombs in the toolshed. The fact that these people can be so swayed by ideology as to abandon the norms by which they have lived in the past suggests a mental imbalance, but one not easily detected.

What goes wrong

Crime stories would come to a halt very quickly if the murderer's plans worked out as intended. One cause of disaster is the expertise of investigators in uncovering clues which the criminal cannot help but leave.

Every criminal leaves a trail in the form of fingerprints, footprints, hairs, sweat and other body fluids, threads from clothing; cars leave tyre-tracks and oil drips. These are obvious and some can be avoided. Less obvious is the evidence of force and direction of blows, and the deduction of a right- or left-handed attacker. Rifling marks on bullets can be matched to the guns which have fired them. Arson rarely goes undetected. Professional thieves develop their own favourite methods of working, by which they can be identified. Even random serial killers can be tracked down through offender profiling.

With so much technology at the disposal of the police, the modern serious crime inquiry is a high-powered affair, using a lot of manpower as well as computers and forensic laboratories. The reading public demands a certain amount of accuracy in the way these large investigations are carried out. It pays for a crime writer to be knowledgeable and their detectives up to date in their methods.

Murderers do not expect to be caught, and go to great lengths to fool the police. They may succeed to some extent, but they are unprepared for the second factor which may wreck their schemes, the unpredictability of their fellow humans. A chance witness, a nosy neighbour, a long-lost cousin or a private detective working for the victim's family can panic a murderer into a second killing which, far from giving protection, actually increases the chance of being caught.

The investigation

There are various ways of presenting the investigation of a crime, the choice being dependent on the character doing the job. If the crime is that of murder, then the police will be investigating, with the other characters as witnesses. The story can be centred on the police; or it may be written from the outside, centred on one or more of the witnesses following, as best they can, what the police are doing. Between these two extremes lie the professional and amateur private detectives, neither of whom has any standing in law other than that of private citizen. This puts them at a disadvantage in relation to the police, unless they are retired officers themselves. They are not likely to be 'called in' to assist in the investigation unless they are respected professional psychologists or forensic scientists occupying professorial Chairs in universities – experts, in other words. An ordinary P.I. would be unlikely to receive much co-operation from the police, but an insurance investigator would stand a good chance.

In suspense novels, the police investigation may be minimal or may not be in progress at all. Then the investigation is most likely to be done by the true amateur, an unwilling detective forced into the job for self-preservation.

Technical aspects of the crime

While there is no need to go into all the gory details of a murder, unless you are so inclined, every crime writer needs to have a minimum of knowledge of ways and means of killing, what to do with the body afterwards, and the sort of evidence furnished by the scene of the crime, the post-mortem on the corpse, and examination of samples taken from both in the forensic laboratory.

It is also necessary to know the general outlines of police procedure: investigation, questioning of witnesses, arrest and remand regulations.

Ways and means of murder

The method is governed largely by the physical circumstances of the crime, and whether or not it is planned in advance or committed on the spur of the moment. A premeditated murder is carefully worked out with a view to concealing the identity of the murderer. An unpremeditated murder leaves the murderer in the awkward predicament of having to think very quickly to cover up clues which will lead the police to him.

The same applies to the type of weapon used. A well-planned murder can be by an obscure weapon, and may be done at a distance, so there are no embarrassing traces of the murderer's own presence at the scene of the crime. A murder provoked by impulse or committed at breaking point is done with any weapon which may be handy, and traces of the murderer's presence – fingerprints, footprints, hairs, dust, shreds from clothing – are inevitable.

Disposal of the body

The choices facing the writer are:

● Leave it where it is. This is by far the easiest, but traces at the scene of the crime may be incriminating.
● Move it to another place to conceal the scene of the crime. This has to be done very quickly if post-mortem staining is not to reveal that the corpse has been moved.
● Throw it, suitably weighted, into river, lake or sea. This will delay investigation. Weighting is not always effective, often inexpertly done, and with no thought to changes to the body and its wrappings during lengthy immersion.
● Bury, or otherwise conceal, it in the countryside. Bodies buried or concealed in undergrowth may not be discovered for years. When they are, identification is very difficult – at times, impossible – and any evidences in soft tissues will have been removed by decomposition and insects. Unless there is evidence from the bones, it will not be possible to establish the cause of death.
● Devise an ingenious way of removing the body alto-

gether. Real-life experience suggests that complicated methods of getting rid of a body are often not as successful as murderers have hoped. Dismembering, acid baths, or even, in one horrific instance, feeding the body to pigs, have not prevented arrest, trial and conviction.

In Appendix I, 'How to Kill Your Victim', you will find detailed notes on a selection of murder methods.

In Appendix II, 'How the Police Operate', you will find a brief description of police organisation, scene-of-crime procedure, CID investigation, the post-mortem examination and the work of the forensic laboratory.

In Appendix III, 'The Legal System in England and Wales', you will find a description of legal procedures on the inquest, arrest, remand and prosecution.

Handling technical data

Ways of using technical data to the writer's advantage include:

- Avoiding 'howlers' through ignorance of procedures.
- Enhancing the credibility of a fictional crime.
- Using forensic high-tech to provide intriguing clues.
- Showing senior police detectives for what they are: highly skilled and intelligent men. They would not be doing the job if they are incompetent.

Sources of information

You will need reliable information on a wide variety of subjects.

Police

Articles about police work appear in the press from time to time. They are written for the general public and are useful to the crime writer. Cut them out and keep them.

Don't hold back from asking the police for details of their organisation within the region where you are setting your novel. Go to the top; don't expect the local PC to be able to help. Write to the Public Relations Officer at Regional Headquarters; he will send you details of what you require.

Pathology

The memoirs of pathologists are mines of information. Both Keith Simpson and Bernard Knight have written excellent books, containing detailed descriptions of cases of special interest.

Consult textbooks. Everything you are likely to need is recorded, and cases are cited from which you may draw material.

Forensic science

For this, too, you must consult textbooks, and make sure that the one you choose is reasonably up to date. A manual of clinical toxicology will tell you about poisons: dosage, lethal levels, symptoms etc.

There are interesting histories of the development of forensic science, which scarcely existed a hundred years ago. These yield a great deal of information as well as fascinating accounts of what has been achieved in various cases.

Firearms are a specialist subject. The main point for the writer is to make sure that the chosen weapon is right for the job it has to do. Fleming made a mistake when he first armed James Bond with a .22; ever afterwards, he consulted his expert. It is advisable to follow his example. Experts are available. Contact a gun club and you will be swept away by an enthusiast who will introduce you to more types of firearm than you knew existed.

Other specialist information

It is highly likely that police and forensic science will not be the only fields in which you need information. Your plot may call for maps; timetables of railways or tides; estimates of length of journeys by road, air or on foot, or your background may need details of some industry or trade. Your characters have their own lives to live. It makes them more interesting if they have some special work or hobby. Being 'something in the City' sounds dull, whereas if a man is a silversmith, or an art collector, or an underwater explorer, something can be made of his profession to enliven the character. He must be the genuine article, and you will have to research his profession or consuming passion to make him so.

Reference libraries are great places for the crime writer, and are usually staffed with willing helpers. If you are intending to write historical crime, that is where you will have to go for your research.

It is a good idea to have your own collection of reference books, works that you will want to keep handy for quick reference. In the Reading List you will find some suggestions.

Developing the plot

Thus far, apart from establishing the theme, we have the crime, the victim, the criminal, the motive, snags in store for the criminal, the investigation, and the technical data. Now we can start developing the plot.

The involvement of the main characters

The building of the characters is discussed at length in Chapter 4. At this stage, the writer is concerned solely with the choice of role for the main characters – the options are: detective; suspect; victim, or criminal. Two of these roles may be combined: for example, a suspect may be obliged to turn amateur detective in order to clear himself; a detective may even turn out to be the murderer.

Other characters

Other characters are required to make the plot work, and the development of the characters will be discussed in the next chapter. At this stage of plotting, all that is required is to know how many characters are needed, and to have a rough idea of their roles. Whatever main roles have not been allocated to the main characters have to be filled; there must be characters to act as red herrings and a few minor characters such as additional police, are needed.

The number of characters should be kept to a minimum, to avoid creating confusion in the reader's mind. Some writers use the device of a 'cast list' in the front of the book to overcome the difficulty. This is a matter of the writer's personal choice, but I think this device should be used sparingly, if at all. The reader may be put off, from the moment of opening the book, by the sight of a long list of characters; and once a reader has been obliged to turn back to the beginning to check on a character, the next action might be to close the book altogether.

Red herrings

The murderer will have made efforts to conceal his guilt, but this is not enough to maintain the suspense. Other characters are set up, in the course of the investigation, as likely murderers. These are red herrings, so called after the fish which used to be dragged across a trail to put off the hounds from following the scent. As the evidence is built up, each red herring is eliminated until, finally, the murderer is caught.

Additional murders

In some circles, it is considered slightly old-fashioned to have more than one murder. I do not go along with this. The number of murders is dictated by the course of the plot. Using extra corpses as space-fillers or to jack up a sagging plot is futile, but additional murders for which there are sound motives are acceptable.

Alibis and clues

The word 'alibi' means 'elsewhere'. The alibi has always been used to place the murderer on the sidelines of the investigation, as an apparently innocent bystander.

Physical and/or psychological clues are present to some degree in all crime novels. They need to be worked out at the planning stage, or you may find that there is not enough evidence to bring home the crime to the murderer.

Worked example – Death Trap II

The theme has provided two main characters: a girl who is alone, and a stranger – an established resident in the neighbourhood. There is a love/hate relationship between them, sparked off by the man's behaviour. The girl is a focus of interest because of the place where she lives and the unsolved deaths of the previous tenants.

So far, these two characters are no more than outlines. That is all that is necessary at this stage of planning, which is concerned with the basic elements of the theme and the plot. The characters will have to be given names, personalities, and backgrounds, in company with whatever other characters the plot will indicate as necessary. This process is described in the next chapter.

The crime

This plot is one where the initial crime, committed by one person, leads to others, committed by somebody else. The background is the impending sale of a medieval painting, which has never before left the family that owns it. Interested parties are: two wealthy art collectors, deadly rivals; and a member of the family who disapproves of the sale of the treasure.

One of the collectors, to make sure of doing down his rival, engages the services of a gang boss to steal the painting before it comes up for sale. This man buys up gambling debts run up by one of the partners in the firm of auctioneers to pressurise him into stealing the painting at the close of the view-day on the day before the sale.

The plan works; the painting is stolen and carried back to the partner's home. He telephones the boss to arrange to hand over the painting, carelessly leaving his front door ajar and the painting on a chair in the hall. When he returns to the hall, it has gone. This makes the partner the first victim. He is questioned with violence by the boss, and dies of a heart attack. The police investigation uncovers evidence pointing to his complicity in the theft, but there is no trace of the painting.

The second theft, from the partner's home, is carried out by a member of the family which owns the painting, who is one of his neighbours. This theft is on impulse, at the sight of the painting in the hall when calling to talk about the sale.

The motive for both thefts is to gain possession of the painting. The police investigation is at a standstill. The insurance company arranges to send one of their investigators to live in the dead man's home (a flat) for a time. This person, a woman, is the second victim. She uncovers the family connection between the second thief and the owners of the painting, and starts inquiries which come to the ears of the second thief, who strikes at once in self-defence and kills the investigator. The police are left with no clues, except that the killer is a professional. They are now convinced that the clue to the whereabouts of the painting must be in the flat, although searches have failed to find it. They arrange for word to be circulated in the art world that the flat is up for letting, and wait to see who takes it.

The new tenant is the girl. Automatically, she is a suspect. But the police plans have gone wrong. Their trap has been sprung by a total innocent, although they, or others interested in the painting, will not believe it.

The development of the plot

This preliminary exploration of the theme and the crime gives pointers for the development of the plot.

● What is the nature of the odd behaviour of the male

main character, and how will he be involved with the crime?

- How has the girl come to obtain the lease of the flat?
- The special characteristics of the murderer: the relationship to the owners of the painting; and the skill as a killer.
- Other characters are indicated: the art collectors, the gang boss, neighbours, police. Also needed are a few outsiders: the girl's friends, and people looking for the painting for their own ends.

All these matters will be dealt with in the next chapter.

Exercise 2

Take any of the themes which you developed from the first ideas of Exercise I. Start devising a plot, following the sequence suggested in this chapter. Take it as far as the stage reached in the worked example.

4

THE CHARACTERS

As the writer considers what characters are needed for working out the plot, ideas of the sort of people required begin to form in the mind.

The theme will have suggested one or two, perhaps more, main characters, but at this early stage, they are little more than types. The development of the plot indicates what other characters are needed – again, by type: the jealous woman; the overbearing father; the Other Woman; the possessive mother; the sweet young innocent girl, the idle son; the macho man; the weakling.

All these types are recognisable, but the human personality is far too complex to be pushed into any category and expected to stay there. Frequently, people do things which surprise those who think they know them best.

For the novelist, types suggested by the plot have to be transformed into credible individuals capable of carrying out the actions required of them.

Sources of characters

The question most frequently asked of writers is: 'Where do the characters come from?' It is followed up by: 'Do you put real people into your books?'

The answer is rarely a straightforward 'A is drawn from Mrs Z; B is a portrait of Mr Y.' Only in the *roman à clef* are the characters deliberately – often maliciously – taken from life and intended to be recognised.

Fictional characters are composites: mixtures of physical and psychological attributes which the creative imagination blends to meet the requirements of any particular plot. The material for this transformation comes from observations of people – their outward appearances, and their mental make-up.

However, these observations provide information only on what the characters look like and what they do. The writer has to provide the motives out of an understanding of the human heart.

Physical observations

In the course of normal living, one encounters a lot of people, all of whom make some sort of impact upon the memory. Everyone is different. Some have outstanding characteristics: good looks, or ugliness; physical peculiarities; ways of walking or talking; nervous habits – all of which are useful to a writer. It is as well to make a practice of observing people, so that the imagination can dredge them up out of the memory as required.

The use of a physical characteristic does not imply that the psychology of the person from whom it is taken is also used for the same character. This might be going a little too near the bone, in risking recognition of the real person. In many cases, the psychology of the subject – a stranger on the street or on public transport – will not be known.

Physical characteristics are used by the novelist to create in the reader an initial response to the character: sympathy, irritation, pity, or antagonism.

Fiction has developed certain clichés: blondes are dumb; heroes are tall, dark and handsome; hunchbacks are devious; villainy shows on the face; liars have shifty eyes. The common experience is that all this is rubbish. These stereotypes have to be avoided. Preferably, they should be turned upside down, to add a little extra punch to the story.

Psychological observations

No academic training is needed to watch how people live their lives, or to work out that most of us are our own worst enemies, and that we bring upon ourselves endless troubles.

By drawing on these observations, the writer can find the psychological make-up of the various characters needed for the plot.

Great care has to be taken over the character of the murderer or other villain. For the purpose of deceiving the reader, it is usually necessary initially to present the villain as a nice person, unveiling his or her true self only at the end. In describing this character, it is essential to include the one characteristic which rational murderers share. This is egoism, an outsize sense of self-importance. To kill another human being to clear them out of one's life, or out of the way of an ambition, is the ultimate ego trip. This holds true even when it is a case of 'the worm turning', when some meek person suddenly lashes out at an oppressor in self-defence. This characteristic will show itself in small ways, even if the person appears benevolent on the surface. In building the character these hints will have to appear, or you may end up with a genuinely charming person who will not make a credible villain.

The other characters, while not criminals, are unlikely to be saints. Give them faults to provide the plot with twists and turns as stress attacks them at their weakest points.

Description of characters

The writer's purpose is to build up in the reader's mind a picture of each character. The actual description does not need to be very detailed. Basically you need to give enough information about the character's physical and mental make-up for the readers to 'see' him for themselves.

If a reader has to keep on turning back to confirm or rediscover who a character is, the fault will lie, most probably, in the initial introduction of that character, which has not been strong enough to fix the character in the reader's mind. The description should stimulate the reader's own imagination to fill in the outline provided by the writer. This helps over the vital matter of 'identification'. The reader should be able to identify with the main character, hero or villain, as the case may be; that is, to take a personal interest in the character.

Physical description

The actual 'look' of a character has to be established quickly, before the wrong mental picture is formed. The problem is that a paragraph of pure description is inappropriate to the desirable pace of a crime novel, especially in the opening pages. A sentence such as: 'Mary was in her early twenties, a girl of middle height, slim, dark, with grey eyes' conveys the necessary information concisely, but it is dull.

Try building the description into the narrative: 'Mary reached up to the top shelf, feeling for a box of matches. She struck one. The small flame lit up a pale, young face framed in dark hair, grey eyes wide in fear: her own reflection in the cracked mirror over the sink. Unnerved, she glanced away quickly, struck another match to look round the kitchen. It burnt her fingers as she stared at the body slumped on the floor. A shudder passed through her slender frame.'

Here, all the information has been crammed into one piece of action. With advantage, it could have been spread over half a page, slotted in where appropriate. The point is that incorporating information into the narrative does not present the reader with the opportunity to skip the paragraph of description; nor does it halt the flow of the action.

Psychological description

A paragraph of description of the psychology of a character would be even less appropriate than one of the physical appearance. Nothing could be more boring than an analysis of various neuroses. The psychology of each character has to be revealed through that character's actions, their reactions to the crime, and through the eyes of other characters.

As an example, Mrs Warren is a possessive mother, determined to keep her hold on her son, and defend him from the lures of designing females. The text could run:

Mrs Warren's face lit up as Tom came into the room. 'Well, darling, how did it go?'

Her son dropped into a chair. 'All right,' he muttered, and picked up the evening paper.

'Is that all?' she pouted. 'Tommy, come and tell me all about it.' She patted the cushion of the sofa. 'You know I love to hear how well you did.'

Pippa, her secretary and general dogsbody, caught the last few words as she entered the room with a fresh flower arrangement. She glanced at the young man with a mixture of exasperation and love. She thought: You'll never get away from the old bag until she pops her clogs, which won't be for years unless one of us gives her a helping hand.

Building up the characters

The process of building up the character is an ongoing one. As the book is written, the personality of each character clarifies, sometimes this is referred to as 'the characters taking over'. What actually happens is that as the characters come to life the writer becomes better acquainted with them. This is a natural development, though it can bring snags: at times, characters do unexpected things. What they do is the natural action of the personality the writer has created for them, but it may not fit in with the plot. If this difficulty arises, it has to be faced, and either the plot changed or the character rewritten. If it is left, there will be a false note in the novel.

At times, crime writers are accused of creating only cardboard characters. This charge is made, frequently, against Agatha Christie. In my view, this is unjust. No matter how clever the puzzle of a whodunnit, the novel will not hold up unless the characters can arouse and hold the interest of the readers. Agatha Christie's characterisation is terse, the descriptions sparse, but there is enough there to fix the reader's attention. At first glance the characters may seem to be stereotypes, but this is to fool the reader. The nicest and mildest frequently turn out to be scheming murderers.

Names

The apparently simple task of naming the characters is a
minefield. Names go in and out of fashion. A glance at
infant school registers will show the current favourites; those
of a sixth form will show yesterday's choice; a trip round a
cemetery will yield a harvest of the changing fashions of
past decades.

Names convey a lot to readers, who will have precon-
ceived ideas of the type of name associated with types of
character. Old-fashioned names such as Albert, Millicent,
Cedric or Nellie suggest older characters, who may range
from the stuffy to the disreputable, and, on the whole, are
unsympathetic. Modern names such as Craig, Shawn, Tracy
or Sharon give an impression of youth and adventure, which
is sympathetic. As fashions change, the old names regain
popularity, as shown in the present reflowering of Emma
and Robert. The public attitude to names is influenced
greatly by the world of pop music and television and the
writer cannot hope to keep completely abreast of the
changes. It is recommended that names should be chosen
from the middle ground, those names which recur from one
generation to the next.

Care has to be taken over the following points: no two
characters' names should begin with the same letter of the
alphabet; and names which sound like each other when read
aloud should not be used.

It is very easy to fall into the trap of the same letter or
the same sound. If the mistake is not corrected, confusion
will arise in the reader's mind.

Care has to be taken, also, over the name given to the
murderer. It is quite possible to give away the identity of
the villain from the start by the use of an unsympathetic
name.

Exploring the character

Characters do not appear in a novel like newborn babes –
without a past. For each one, a background has to be
created. It should cover: family circumstances and relation-

ships; how the character sees himself, his lifestyle; the front presented to others; his job and attitude to work; tastes, leisure activities, attitude to the opposite sex, interests.

The point of this is to get to know the character 'in the round'. A good deal of the information may not appear in the text. It is part of the substructure of the novel essential to the writer, who must have a fundamental understanding of the characters if they are to take on life for the readers.

Special cases

In creating the background for a contemporary character in a Western European setting, the writer is able to draw upon personal knowledge and experience. It is a different matter when the character belongs to another culture or another period.

Outside our own culture, which embraces the Americas, and places settled by Europeans, lies the rest of the world: the Levant, Asia, the Far and the Middle East, Africa. It is a mistake to imagine that, because many of these places were under colonial rule, our Western culture has made any marked impact on the indigenous population.

These areas are very different from our own in terms of social structures, philosophies and religions, and ways of life. Crossing cultural divides is difficult. Empire-builders of the last century did not try; nor, regrettably, did many of the missionaries. Now that the colonial regimes have all but vanished, and the churches are run by native clergy, the old culture, customs and ways of thought have risen to the surface once more.

These places make wonderful, exotic backgrounds for crime stories, but most are written with Westerners as the main characters, and only a sprinkling of the country's nationals in supporting roles of police, doctors, lawyers and servants. In these days of mass travel and communication, it would be a crass mistake to portray such characters as buffoons. The professional classes and those who have made profitable careers out of serving Western expatriates have absorbed a great deal of Western culture, and maintain standards long since fallen into decay in the West. But this applies only to a small section of the population. The majority have never changed their ways, save in the most superficial manner. It would require a person of extraordinary perception to be able to write convincingly about them after spending only a short holiday in the country.

An outstanding example of writing successfully about an Eastern culture is the work of James Melville. His novels feature Superintendent Tetsuo Otani and members of his squad of detectives. The idea of writing about a Japanese detective would daunt most people, but Melville worked in Japan for a number of years, and knows what he is writing about. The character of Otani has been drawn from life, and is based on a number of Japanese officials with whom he had dealings.

The Japanese appear to be highly conscious of the cultural collision between themselves and the West, to which they have an ambivalent attitude. This is reflected in the character of Otani. He is of an age to have seen service as a very junior officer in Naval Intelligence at the end of the war; he is conservative, old-fashioned, wary of foreigners. He has a liberal background – in Japanese terms – his father being a professor who got into trouble with the authorities during the war. He loves the old way of life, and the elaborate courtesies, which are evident even in the everyday bustle of his office. At the same time, he is astute, and, although he does not understand the Westerners who come his way, they do not get the better of him. Otani is a rounded and convincing character. I recommend a study of him.

Historical characters

Historical crime presents different difficulties. It can be set in any age, any culture. Some writers use actual historical figures; others create fictional characters to fit in with the period. The real-life character is someone who has made a mark in the world, and about whom a fair bit is known. This is a help, but it also imposes certain restrictions. For a fictional character, the writer can create whatever sort of person they choose, as long as the details of everyday life and contemporary ideas are correct.

Except for very remote periods, plenty of resource material is available, both written and pictorial. From the seventeenth century on, there are diaries, letters and memoirs; later on, newspapers and magazines become available.

Writing the characters into the plot

The assembling of the cast of characters goes hand in hand with the development of the plot. It is most unlikely that the whole cast will have appeared in the earliest stage of planning.

In the two previous chapters, the theme has been established and the crime described. Now we have the starting point: the main and minor characters are already involved, and there is some idea of how the plot will develop. This process is demonstrated in the worked example.

Worked example – Death Trap III

Refer back to *Death Trap I* (Chapter 2) which provided the first two main characters, the girl and the man; and also the theme of self-development (of the girl). Refer also to *Death Trap II* (Chapter 3) which provided the crime, the criminals, and the pointers for development of the plot. Now the characters must be added.

Main characters

THE GIRL, LORNA GARRETT: age 22; pretty, blonde, average height; lively, intelligent (holds a degree in Fine Arts); sees herself as confident and capable of looking after herself. English, but has lived in New York for several years with an aunt (see below), who took her in after the death of her mother. Her father works in the Third World, does not come home often. The aunt is an antique dealer, and has sent Lorna to London to learn the British end of the trade. Lorna loves her work, is eager to learn, and is delighted at her trip to Europe; she is ready to have fun.

THE MAN, THEO RANDALL: reclusive bachelor of 38;

scholarly; awkward with women; art historian and curator of a private collection; has been asked by the insurance company to watch the new tenant of the flat; fancies himself as a detective, having helped them out on a few occasions; does not know what to make of Lorna, is surprised at the effect she has on him, is reluctant to believe her to be the associate of thieves and murderers although the evidence suggests she is; steels himself against her; does his job by acting the helpless male, constantly running to her with small domestic problems. He is tall, dark, not handsome, wears baggy trousers and jackets.

Criminals

GANG BOSS, CHARLIE HACKETT: specialises in art and antique thefts and smuggling. Rarely seen in public. Elderly and ruthless.

GANG MEMBERS: Two young thugs, handy with knives and other 'persuaders'; and a woman, smart and respectable looking, who 'fronts' for Hackett.

THE CLIENT, MICHAEL PANACLOS: Greek shipping tycoon, art collector not above acquiring works of art he dare not admit to having. Middle-aged, reclusive, surrounds himself with bodyguards and secretaries.

HACKETT'S THIEF, CHAPMAN: partner in fine art salesroom; gambler; lives alone, wife left him over constant quarrels over money; accepts Hackett's offer in desperation over debts; hopes to bluff his way out of police questioning, fails to convince Hackett that the painting was stolen from him.

THE SECOND THIEF/MURDERER, MARGUERITE ENGLISH: neighbour of Chapman; formidable, tall, mannish, very fit despite being in her seventies; illegitimate daughter of English duke and Frenchwoman, bitterly resentful of treatment by her father's family; detested by them for many reasons, the main one the fortune left her by her father; heroine of French Resistance during the war, where she learnt how to kill, make bombs and other unladylike skills; married after war, husband disappeared long ago; has one son, Brian; never speaks about her family or her heroic past.

Investigators

CHIEF SUPERINTENDENT SOUTHAM: very senior officer, specialist on art theft and fraud. Large, formidable-looking man.

PENELOPE BOLAND: experienced insurance investigator. Mid-forties. Not tall, but capable of defending herself against any ordinary assault. No match for Mrs English. On uncovering the family connection, suspects Brian of stealing the painting from Chapman.

Other characters

BRIAN ENGLISH: neighbour; tall, fair, the image of his ducal grandfather; unmarried, forty; engineer, away on business a lot; disapproves of mother's obsession over family; falls in love with Lorna at first sight, but diffident in approaching her (mother would disapprove).

DAPHNE FITZROY: neighbour; elderly widow, fluffy and still pretty; kind; devoted to Mrs English.

IRENE ALDERLEY: Greek, married to Englishman; smart, fiftyish; husband retired; socialite.

MILDRED GARRETT: Lorna's aunt (already mentioned above); highly respected in top-class antique trade; lives in New York; asked London friends to look out for a flat for Lorna.

JOSEPH MARCUS: friend of Mildred Garrett; old and respected antique dealer, with a shop in Bond Street; has agreed to take Lorna as an apprentice for six months.

FREDDIE TEMPLETON: friend of Mildred Garrett; slightly shady antique dealer with shop in Chelsea; late forties, but makes himself seem younger; sharp dresser; bright and amusing; presents a light and charming veneer to the world; unscrupulous; seizes on Mildred's request to find a flat for Lorna as the ideal method of gaining access, through her, to Chapman's flat, to hunt for clues to whereabouts of painting, and earn large reward offered by insurance company.

PHILIP DADURIAN: Armenian tycoon, Panaclos's rival in business and art collecting; long-term liaison with Mildred Garrett; Lorna regards him as a substitute father.

EVE SIMMONDS, known as 'FRIDAY': South African, distant relation of Dadurian; enterprising young woman out for adventure, with some experience of art fraud and theft; early thirties, very glamorous, ash-blonde; persuades Dadurian to back her in looking for the painting; charms Freddie into taking her on as temporary assistant, while they both hunt for it.

Roles

All the necessary characters are now assembled, taking into account the pointers to the development of the plot from the previous worked example *Death Trap II*. The next stage is to assign to each character a specific role.

LORNA: an innocent person involved in a mystery she does not understand; distrusts Randall and the police; trusts Freddie Templeton and Eve Simmonds.

RANDALL: suspects Lorna from the start, reluctantly comes round to her support.

SOUTHAM: Satisfied that he has the right mouse in his trap; waits for Lorna to lead him to the painting and the murderer.

MRS ENGLISH: has no fear that she will be suspected;

keeps an eye on Lorna; prepared to strike the moment she scents danger.

FREDDIE TEMPLETON: two-faced, presents himself as Lorna's friend, but is only using her as a means to get at the painting.

EVE 'FRIDAY' SIMMONDS: working primarily for herself and DADURIAN, using both Freddie and Lorna.

HACKETT AND GANG: assume Lorna holds key to whereabouts of painting, and act accordingly. Their main function in the plot is to keep the reader's attention on the motive for the original theft, and the rivalry between Panaclos and Dadurian.

PANACLOS, DADURIAN, JOSEPH MARCUS AND IRENE ALDERLEY will be used as red herrings.

The work of developing the plot is suspended, at this point, to discuss the ways of handling the settings of a crime novel in the next chapter. It will be resumed in Chapter 6, when the various scenes of action have been worked out.

Exercise 3

Work out what characters you will need for your own plot. Write biographical notes about them, describe them in detail, and decide what role each will play.

5

THE SETTING

The setting in a novel is, to use theatrical terminology, the stage on which the plot is acted out. The word 'stage' is important. The setting should have its own part to play in the plot, and not be used merely as a backdrop.

Describing the setting

Settings cover everything from the geographical position, down through town and village, to specific houses, and even rooms; all need to be fixed in the reader's mind.

Home setting – urban

When writing about England, for a largely British readership, minimal description will suffice for a plot set, for example, in London. The readers can relate to London in a special way. They are used to reading and seeing on television a lot about London. They are familiar with how it looks; in the centre; the crowded streets of the East End; the affluence of Belgravia, Chelsea, and Hampstead; the suburban sprawl of the outer areas. The same applies, to a lesser extent, to the other major cities. No one needs to be told about the nature of our cities, the way they contain all different social groups, the sort of life lived in them.

What has to be done is to pinpoint in which layer of urban society the action takes place and whatever else is necessary to the plot to fix the setting in the writer's mind so that the various scenes of action may ring true.

A description of the architecture and layout of the street and property in which scenes are set is usually enough, and feeds the general opinions of what these are like in the various social strata in this country.

Home setting – rural

There is a general conception of a 'typical' English village which does not take into account the fact that this sort of village exists only in the areas where large-scale arable farming has been carried out for centuries. Hilly areas have small, scattered settlements due to the use of land largely for sheep farming. Surprising as it may seem in an apparently overcrowded country, there are still large tracts of wild, inhospitable land in Britain with isolated homesteads, and harsh working conditions. To deal with these areas, it is necessary to create new images for the urban readers.

Writers using these places as settings must be aware that the scattered inhabitants all know each other; that there is more social contact than might be imagined; and that everything that happens is noted and reported.

The general tenor of rural life is on the old-fashioned side: people still hunt, shoot and fish, live in freezing houses, and wrest a living from the land, albeit with machines when they can afford them.

The country towns present much the same pattern. They, too, depend on agriculture for supplies, services, markets etc. The inhabitants not only know each other but are inter-related, a fact which police posted from an urban area to a rural one frequently find difficult to understand.

With the bulk of the population – and therefore the readership – living in cities, writers using rural settings need to take care to give as accurate as possible a picture of the different way of life.

Foreign setting

In using a foreign setting, it has to be assumed that the reader is unfamiliar with the chosen location, even if it is as well known as Paris or Rome. In an alien environment, the basic features of the setting have to be established quickly.

Geographically, the setting has to be identified on the first page, and described in minimum terms to start creating the picture in the reader's mind. Further description can be added, bit by bit, as the need arises.

The first task, then, is to decide what must accurately give the flavour of the setting. Some writers claim that they do not need to visit a location they intend to use as a setting, but can obtain all that they require from guidebooks. Most of us have to do it the hard way, foot-slogging through some hot and sticky town to gain first-hand impressions of the place.

In using a foreign setting, all the things we take for granted at home – the way of life and its tempo; the climate; social attitudes; how people amuse themselves – have to be looked at with inquiring eyes. Even if the main characters are all British, they cannot be kept immune from the local community and its customs. In a crime book, it is unlikely that they will be able to avoid the attentions of the local police force.

Moving out of Europe, the whole local culture will be quite different from our own. Where this problem is overcome, the books are intensely interesting apart from whatever crime is involved.

A Western European, arriving for a first visit to a Third World country, experiences a considerable shock. If it is in daylight, there is a blast of heat and glare, and colours of an unimagined brilliance. If the arrival is at night, one steps out into a hot, fragrant darkness, noisy with crickets – and then starts swatting mosquitoes homing in on nice fresh flesh.

Example of setting notes

Here is an extract from notes I made while in Pointe Noire, a port in what used to be the French Congo, now the People's Republic of the Congo:

- A straggling town, with an immense sweep of beach on

either side of the point. European quarter, houses set in gardens with many trees; native quarter, unpaved streets of small houses, with shared standpipes for water supply; port busy but inefficient, always a queue of ships out to sea, waiting to unload; special pier for loading potash, deserted, unused. Run-down town, wide streets full of potholes.

- Many French residents, who have stayed on after Independence. Good hotel, and two or three excellent restaurants and bars, fresh supplies flown in from Paris every week; clientèle the expatriates and well-off Congolese. Most of native population live no better than under colonial rule.

- Main boulevard, running straight from the railway station and the imposing Post Office, decorated with flags faded to pink with symbol of hammer and mattock, favourite racetrack of police/army in jeeps blowing whistles as they go. Statue of ex-colonial bigwig now daubed with graffiti.

- Working life: port area full of offices, half-asleep under trees; women do all manual work, even log-chopping; men beginning to work in small industries, good carpenters; grandiose schemes for industrialisation, e.g. digging potash, which come to little or nothing; tailors set up their sewing machines under the trees waiting for customers; women sit on the ground selling bananas and bread.

- French residents lead the good life – lives of leisure for the women spent in golf, riding, bridge; club life in the evening, or dining out at restaurants with tables under the trees.

- Poverty and unemployment among the Congolese; squatters live on the beach; blind beggars led by others who can see in front of the European-style shops and the hotels; burglaries common, accompanied by horrible violence.

- Most buildings fairly modern; some old houses survive as schools or offices.

- Climate equatorial, cooled by nearness of sea and cold current, very humid; an astonishing range of insects, huge mosquitoes; huge landcrabs; turtles.

- Communications: rail link to capital; most people use the air service (small planes, sometimes cargo ones).
- Surrounding countryside scrubby vegetation, sandy tracks, rivers dangerous (alligators, their tails a local delicacy), beautiful beaches, warm sea.

These notes came from my own observations, and therefore were external. Accurate information about the attitudes of the indigenous population never came my way. French colonials never drew apart from the natives the way the British usually did, but it was difficult to meet ordinary Congolese, my contacts being business associates and government officials – all educated people with French habits. Books written by one-time colonel officials or missionaries can help bridge the gap. Less helpful are the horror stories about workmen and servants told by expatriates, which are likely to be exaggerated.

First impressions may not be accurate, but can be checked by reading guidebooks, travellers' tales, and the local newspapers. This last may present language difficulties, but major centres usually have English-language newspapers on sale.

Checklist for location work

- Record everything that strikes you. Do not try to remember it all. Write it down.
- Analyse your own first impressions: light, colours, climate, noise, scents, the expressions of people in the streets, traffic.
- How do people live – in houses, apartments, huts?
- Are the ordinary police militarised, carrying guns?
- What sort of life is lived?
- Take photographs of everything, to jog your memory later.
- Buy maps and plans of town and countryside; get hold of timetables for buses, trains, ferries, tides.
- What is the countryside like – vegetation, crops, hills, rivers and so on?
- Write descriptions of things not normally recorded – early mornings, sunsets, processions, family outings.

70

● Find out what flowers and trees are in bloom at which time of the year. What sort of gardens do people have?

Remember: until you start writing, you never know exactly what you will need by way of local colour to integrate the plot into the setting. It is better to make notes on too much rather than too little.

If possible, make a second visit when you are well on with writing the book.

Detailed settings

The geographical location gives only a general picture, aimed at creating atmosphere. The sites of the action – homes, public places, streets – require greater detail.

Street layouts and domestic architecture vary widely even within one country. These regional variations are generally the product of the particular history of the place, the type of building materials available in days before mass transport, and the common means of earning a living in time past. The changes brought about in modern times do not greatly alter the old pattern, except for the building of ever-larger roads.

Great differences are visible inside the home, and the way that rooms are used. In England, there is no standard use of our living space, as differences in class often dictate this. The same is true of much of Western Europe. Further afield, the homes themselves are different.

Plans

Drawing plans of the layout of houses, streets and public places such as railway stations may assist you in working details of the plot. It is not recommended to leave them in the typescript. In the 1930s whodunnits very often contained plans, so that the reader might understand the nature of an alibi and see how it had been rigged, or why some character was lying in claiming to have seen another at a particular place. The fashion may return in the future, but for the moment, it is rarely used. The great argument against it is

71

that it is a bad idea to give the reader occasion to leave off reading and turn back to the plan to verify a point. In most contemporary work, the writer aims to give all the necessary information in the text itself.

Historical settings

With the current popularity for historical crime stories, it is worth spending a moment on the special needs of their settings.

Research is a necessity, but it does not have to be from primary sources. There are good scholarly transcriptions of a host of medieval documents, from *The Anglo-Saxon Chronicle* and the Domesday Book onwards. There are excellent books written by social historians describing life, manners, customs, everyday objects, household management, sports, leisure and travel in earlier ages.

Major reference libraries hold newspapers and magazines on microfilm; collections of letters, diaries and pictures, the Victoria County Histories, and Transactions of History and County societies are all good sources of detail.

In many old towns, lists of ratepayers have survived, showing the houses they occupied. Old maps of towns also survive. Features shown on them, long since obliterated, can be identified in old street names, for example Parson's Glebe; Sheep Market; Doctor's Piece; Widow's Orchard. There are many clues to follow up, even in fairly remote periods, to create the proper atmosphere.

For her Brother Cadfael stories, Ellis Peters has used a well-documented setting. All that remains of Shrewsbury Abbey now is the church, and its lands are all built over, but the roads follow the old courses, and if the bridge is new, the centre of the town is still caught in the noose of the Severn which made it a defensible site from earliest times. It does not take a great deal of imagination to see abbey and town as they were in the Middle Ages.

Peter Lovesey sets his crime stories in the late nineteenth century, when London had had a proper police force for half a century, and had developed a detective force. He creates his settings with loving care, the keynote being accuracy of detail, from Sergeant Cribb's twopenny pint of ale after knocking off work to chasing villains on a tricycle commandeered from a country policeman. In *The Detective Wore Silk Drawers*, setting and plot are interdependent. The crime arises out of a late nineteenth-century situation: illegal, and highly profitable bare-knuckle prize-fighting, with the detectives chasing over fields and tracks after crowds of supporters making furtively for the secret venues. In creating his settings, Lovesey takes care that his period details are not obtrusive, but fit naturally into the narrative. The main drive of the story comes first. Period details are secondary to it and nothing extra can be put in. Details which do not fit into the story or move it on should not be put in. If the reader's attention is caught by the details rather than by the story, the setting has been overdone.

The time of year

No setting can be described successfully without reference to the season of the year. Flowers bloom at different times; trees change colour; rivers run high or dry. The atmosphere of places changes with the seasons. Grey, windswept hills look quite different when covered with sheep; in spring sunshine, old houses are suddenly less gloomy. It was not for nothing that so many old stories began: 'It was a dark and stormy night . . .'

Be definite about the time of year in which the action takes place. It is bound to have a bearing on your crime. In winter, long hours of darkness or difficulty in summoning aid due to storms or sheer distance will hinder an investigation. In summer, people will be out and about quite late in the evening, so perhaps there will be more witnesses, if not to the crime itself, to the establishment or breaking of alibis.

Place names

The question is always whether to use real names or not. This should depend on whether or not the use of an actual name may cause distress or stir up trouble.

There is little point to inventing names for major countries, their capitals and principal cities. Their scale is large enough to have room for a corner of fictional criminal activity without the author running the risk of accusations of besmirching their fair name.

On the other hand, it may well be advisable to give invented names to small and emerging countries with hypersensitive governments, especially as the thrust of the novel might be slightly uncomplimentary in painting the place in its true colours rather than those of the tourist brochures. This is entirely a matter of personal choice.

Where a small town or village is used as a setting, a real one, with a suitably disguised name, may be used. More commonly, a fictitious one is created, to give the writer greater freedom to make of it whatever is needed for the story. In creating such a town or village, care has to be taken that it has the outward appearance general to the region in which it is set – built of stone, brick, or half-timbered; with a wide main street or a maze of alleys – so that it will ring true. The invented name, too, will need to sound likely.

Working the setting into the plot

Within the general geographical setting, the action will move from place to place, even if only between different parts of a building. No two of these places will be identical. Each has its individual features which will need to be worked out. This can be used to advantage in revealing facets of the personality of various characters: for example, in any house, the decor and furnishings bear the imprint of the owner's individuality.

To have all this clear in the mind, the various scenes need to be treated in the same manner as the characters, with detailed notes to help you commit to memory everything that lies within the setting. When writing is in progress, the important points will be selected and used. In this process, the nature of the scenes may suggest improvements or alternatives to the action you have in mind. These second thoughts are always worth considering.

Worked example – Death Trap IV

Setting: General – London
    Detailed – a block of flats in an upmarket suburb.

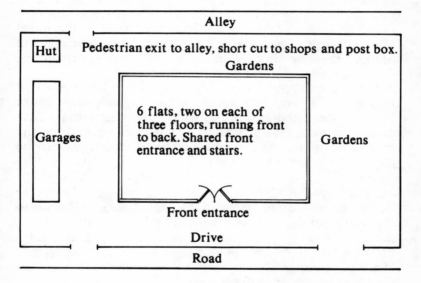

Occupants: Ground floor – Mrs English, Mrs Fitzroy; first floor – Brian English, Mr and Mrs Alderley; top floor – Theo Randall, Chapman (later Mrs Boland, Lorna)
    The hut is the place where the maintenance man keeps tools, lawnmowers etc.
    The alley is where Mrs Boland's body was found.
    The flats are owner-occupied and expensive.

Interiors

Scenes are set in all the flats except that of the Alderleys.

Chapman
Functional rather anonymous furnishings. Not what might be expected of the home of a man in the Fine Arts world, suggesting that he has other uses for money than buying fine furniture or pictures – perhaps a costly habit, such as gambling. Only the collection of books reveals his interest in his job.

Randall
Fine furniture and beautiful objects; overflowing with books; scholarly atmosphere.

Mrs English
Heavy, good furniture, severe style. A few good pictures but few pretty things, and no fripperies. Large and heavily gilded mirror over hall table. Mementoes of her wartime work hidden in a box in her wardrobe. The only photograph is a studio portrait of her son, Brian.

Mrs Fitzroy
A motley collection of small pieces of antique furniture, favourites selected to bring with her when she moved to the flat from a large house she and her husband had lived in until his death. Many photographs of family and friends. Hosts of ornaments, many kept for sentimental reasons. Pot plants to brighten up the place.

Brian English
Flat furnished by his mother to suit her own austere taste. Personal touches added by photographs and books. The kitchen is well equipped, betraying an interest in gourmet cookery.

Other settings

Mr Marcus's shop in Bond Street
Very high-class antiques. The building is narrow and goes

back to an alley. Behind the shop itself is the office, then a small kitchen, with a back door to a yard where the dustbin is kept.

Freddie Templeton's shop in Chelsea
A rung or two lower than Mr Marcus's business.
  Freddie deals in anything that brings in good prices, including Art Deco and old telephones.

Philip Dadurian's house in Belgravia
Very grand, and furnished to match.
  London streets, gardens, taxis, police stations do not need special description.

Time of year:
Winter to Early spring

Place names
No need to change the name of the general location, the suburb can remain anonymous. Bond Street and Chelsea are well enough known to need no change.
  Special item: There is one object, so far undescribed except in the most general terms – the missing picture. It is a 15th-century work on two hinged wooden panels. Folded, it will fit into a briefcase. It is known as the Roxton Diptych, painted in Flanders in 1470 by the Master of Maldeghem, on the occasion of the marriage of the Duke of Roxton to a Flemish lady, whose portraits the two panels bear.

Exercise 4

Work out your settings, describing in detail to familiarise yourself with them; decide on the time of year and how this will influence the action; invent what place names you need.

6

THE PLOT NARRATIVE

The preliminary preparations are now complete: the crime and its motive have been worked out; the characters assembled; the setting and the scenes within it visualised. The next stage is to put together all this material to form a continuous narrative of the plot.

The sequence of the action provides the framework. To it will be added: the characters involved at each stage; development of how and why the finger of suspicion points at those designated as red herrings; and the clues which will reveal the identity of the criminal.

At each stage of compiling the plot narrative, the corresponding stage in the worked example will be shown as illustration. The action will be shown in roman type and the commentary – reasons, reactions, etc. – in italics.

The origins of the crime

This is the starting point. The roots of the crime, no matter how deep or far back, provide the impetus for the commission of the crime.

This does not mean that the book will have to start at this point. The choice of where to start is of vital importance, and will be discussed in Chapter 7.

Worked example – Death Trap V(a)

- Duke of Roxton decides to send painting to auction to pay death duties, estimated price £750,000. *Mrs English is horrified. Was her father's favourite picture. Wonders if she could raise enough to buy it. Dadurian and Panaclos both want it.*

- Panaclos engages Hackett to steal painting before sale, for fee of £250,000. *Hackett puts pressure on Chapman (partner in saleroom), holds IOU for large gambling debt. Chapman yields to pressure to clear debt.*

The commission of the crime

This is a technical matter involving the methods by which the crime is committed; the efforts, if any, made to cover tracks; traces left at the scene of the crime; the results of post-mortem examinations and forensic laboratory tests; the witnesses; the initial direction of suspicion.

Worked example – Death Trap V(b)

- Theft carried out on view-day. Painting taken out in briefcase. Chapman goes home to phone Hackett. Omits to shut front door, expecting to go straight out again. *A porter notices Chapman's briefcase looks fatter than usual.*
- Mrs English follows Chapman up to flat. *She has been to the view-day, discovers Chapman works at salesroom, hears him come home, goes up to ask him how much the painting is likely to fetch.*
- Mrs English sees painting in open briefcase on hall table, takes it, slips back downstairs. Conceals it behind mirror in her own hall. *Motive: to save it from the thief; keeps it to punish family.*
- Hackett does not believe Chapman's story, seizes him, tries torture to get truth out of him. Chapman dies of heart attack. Body dumped. *Chapman has no idea who can have stolen it. No one at flats knows of Mrs English's connection with the Roxtons.*
- CS Southam open police inquiry. Comes up with no leads. Search of flat yields no clues. *Evidence from sales-*

room points to Chapman as thief. Body found, shows traces of torture.

In the worked example, this completes the first section of the plot narrative. The police investigation moves away from the block of flats and its occupants, and concentrates on underworld contacts. Since that element has very little bearing on this plot, there is going to be a time lag in the action which will create a problem when planning the book.

Time lags

In real-life police investigations, time lags are the norm. In fiction, they have to be dealt with in some way which will hold the reader's interest. In a police procedural novel, a time lag in one investigation gives room for following the investigation of one of the other crimes featured. In a novel concentrating upon one crime, or series of crimes, this is not possible, and other devices have to be used such as: prologues; dividing up the plot into the different times of action; using the gap to develop the reactions of witnesses; or making the starting point of the novel a place where time lags have finished, and the action can proceed at a good pace, incorporating the earlier history of the crime into the background.

Time lags need to be marked in the plot narrative, to avoid any possible confusion which might pass unnoticed under the pressure of the actual writing of the book. Confusion in the mind of the author is communicated to the reader very quickly.

Worked example – Death Trap V(c)

- Time lag one month.
- Insurance company plants investigator, Penelope Boland, in Chapman's flat. *Boland is playing a hunch that Chapman had one of his neighbours as an accomplice.*

- Brian English comes home for weekend. Boland sees him. *Boland spots Brian English's likeness to Roxtons.*
- Boland makes discreet inquiries about Brian. *She picks on Mrs Fitzroy as most likely to gossip. She suspects Brian was Chapman's accomplice.*
- Mrs Fitzroy mentions this to Mrs English. *Immediately, Mrs English understands the danger.*

Dealing with snags

In every crime story, something happens to prevent the criminal from getting away with his crime. These snags have to be dealt with as soon as the villain becomes aware of them. Defensive action is called for: an additional crime, or the hasty fabrication of an alibi may be necessary. Whatever it is, this action will be fraught with danger to the criminal, since there is little or no time for careful preparation.

The defensive action is likely to be more drastic than is actually necessary. This takes into account the element of shock to the criminal, who has been feeling safe. If further snags appear, possibly as a result of the defensive action, shock will turn into panic. That is the point at which the villain will start making the serious mistakes which will lead to his/her downfall.

Worked example – Death Trap V(d)

- Mrs English watches Boland, follows her when she goes out in evening (dark) to postbox in alley. Strangles her. *During war, she learnt killing techniques, and knows that survival depends on bold action when threatened.*
- Body left in alley. *Attempt to make it look like a mugging.*
- Mrs English takes handbag (contains key to flat). Hides it in her wardrobe.
- Southam investigates murder. *Only one clue: killing an expert job. Southam concludes Boland had got on track of painting. Clue to whereabouts must be in flat.*
- By arrangement with Chapman's executors, Southam

sets a trap, circulating the rumour in Fine Arts circles that the flat is to let. He waits to see who takes it.

Reactions of other characters

The criminal's defensive action has repercussions upon the other people involved, however marginally, with the crime. Those who feel threatened by it will take steps to secure their own position; others may try to take advantage of it in furthering some project of their own, and some may see an opportunity of making mischief.

All these actions complicate the issue, make the task of the investigator more difficult, and may, or may not, be of help to the criminal. They form sub-plots.

Sub-plots

Sub-plots are inevitable because a character who exists solely in relation to the crime can never be more than a cardboard cutout. Each character in any novel is pursuing their own interests, and their reaction to the crime will be governed by the extent to which it affects those interests.

Sub-plots are useful in providing red herrings, or other means of diverting the attention of the reader, such as dealing with love affairs, successful or otherwise; disrupting plans of criminals; and humanising detectives. They need careful handling, since a sub-plot cannot be gone into in great detail without upsetting the balance of the novel. All that is necessary is enough for the sub-plot to do its job within the framework of the main plot.

Worked example – Death Trap V(e)

● Dadurian commissions a freelance investigator, Eve Simmonds, to take over Boland's task. *Simmonds eager to collect reward for finding painting as well as fee.*

● Simmonds invites antique dealer, Freddie Templeton,

to work with her and share reward. *Freddie keen. She does not tell him of her connection with Dadurian.*

- Freddie remembers American friend, Mildred Garrett, has asked him to find a flat for her niece, Lorna. He and Simmonds concoct a plan to use Lorna as a means of getting into Chapman's flat to search it. He obtains the lease of the flat for Lorna.

- Lorna Garrett arrives from New York to work as a trainee for six months with antique dealer Joseph Marcus. She moves into the flat. *Freddie befriends her; other residents welcome her; Brian falls in love with her. No one tells her about the deaths of Chapman and Boland, or about the loss of the painting.*

- Freddie puts out a rumour that the new tenant of Chapman's flat is a girl called Eve, who knows where the painting is. *Lorna is being set up to receive unwelcome attention from interested parties which will frighten her into accepting Simmonds as a live-in companion. Simmonds insists on using her own name (Eve) so that Dadurian will assume she is the actual tenant, and will make sure his own people will leave her alone. Freddie is willing to go along with anything she says. Simmonds is unaware of Dadurian's connection with Lorna, as is Freddie.*

- Insurance company engages Randall to watch Lorna. He is given a key to the flat to search it when the opportunity arises. *Randall fancies himself as a detective, having helped a few times. He assumes Lorna is working for someone looking for the painting.*

- Hackett picks up the rumour about the new tenant. *He assumes she has taken the flat to pick up a clue left for her by Chapman to retrieve the painting from the place where he hid it. Has her watched.*

- CS Southam puts a tail on Lorna. *He thinks he has found Chapman's accomplice, who has come to retrieve the painting and hand it on to the final customer. He regards her innocent routine as mere caution. He is willing to play a waiting game.*

At this point in the plot narrative, the sub-plots have emerged. They are:

- Eve Simmonds and Freddie Templeton hoping to earn money.
- Hackett still anxious to earn his fee for obtaining the painting for Panaclos.
- Randall trying to recover the painting before it disappears into a secret collection.
- Dadurian anxious to foil his rival's plans if at all possible.

Further development of the plot

Every turn of the plot needs to rest on a solid basis of logical sequence: action and reaction, as each character pursues their own way through the difficulties. Care has to be taken that these responses are within the psychological make-up you are creating for each character, yet it is important to remember that people react unpredictably when put under stress. Some keep their heads, others go to pieces, and many blunder about in a well-meaning fashion and frequently make matters worse. No one is likely to act normally, but the reactions you write for each character will highlight their strengths and their weaknesses, and strip off many a polite veneer.

By this stage, the main lines of the story are laid down, and the roles of most of the characters indicated. Before proceeding further, work out your various devices for keeping the suspense going, throwing dust in the eyes of the reader and concealing the identity of the criminal until the moment of revelation.

Alibis

Alibis are tight constructions depending largely on time and place, supported by outside witnesses, or the restrictions imposed by travel from one place to another.

The best sort of outside witness is a character of good reputation, whose word most people, even the police, are willing to accept. These alibis can be demolished by proving, in the course of the action, that the witness is not disinterested, and may be part of a neat little conspiracy.

An alternative version of this sort of alibi is where two possible suspects alibi each other. This is much more shaky, and both the alibis fall to pieces if one does not stand up to scrutiny.

Alibis based on timetables rest on the physical impossibilities either of being in two places at once, or of travelling from A to B in less than a certain time. Fictional murderers often make short work of these difficulties. In Dorothy Sayer's *The Five Red Herrings*, the murderer is seen to board a train and can establish his presence at its destination later in the day. The trick is that he leaves the train immediately on boarding by a door on the opposite side, crosses the tracks, picks up a stashed bicycle, pedals off to kill his victim, and then continues his journey.

False alibis are open to the danger of the unexpected event, some happening which the subject would know about had they really been where they pretend they were.

Innocent suspects can be in difficulties, because often people have no idea where they were at any particular time. Readers are well aware of this, so it is somewhat dangerous to make the only character with a respectable-sounding alibi the villain; the show may be given away too soon.

Red herrings

The purpose of red herrings is to misdirect the attention of the reader. However, there has to be a good, logical reason for suspicion to fall upon these characters. This will arise from the circumstances, or through misinterpretations of their own actions, or through deliberate attempts to throw suspicion upon them by any of the other characters, for any amount of reasons.

In creating red herring characters, allowance must be made for the element of shock. They know they are innocent, and the last thing in the world they expect is to be accused of some crime. They will be appalled, and will show this in the range of their emotions, from righteous rage to helpless tears. What they do to defend themselves is likely to be inspired by panic, and will probably prove ineffective.

A red herring character may be vindicated by the unexpected production of a sound alibi, or he may have to wait until the final solution to be cleared.

Worked example – Death Trap V(f)

In this plot, there is little use of alibis. This is because the crimes are not dependent upon the whereabouts of any particular character at a certain time. Essentially, the crimes are crude, opportunistic.

Chapman, in stealing the painting, is intending to bluff his way out of awkward questions, relying upon the fact that the salesroom is milling with people on the view-day. His intention is to take the line that anyone could have removed the painting, which is small enough to be easily concealed. It is an important item, but not the only one: a large collection of good paintings is on sale. He is relying on the fact that it will have left his possession almost before the alarm is raised. He assumes that no one knows of his gambling debts, so no motive could be attributed to him; this shows him as an amateur, certain to be caught.

Mrs English tackles criminal activity with the professionalism she learnt in underground fighting, and does not do anything more than what is absolutely necessary to protect herself. She relies on the fact that she is unlikely to attract any police attention, and is secure in the knowledge that no one knows of her connection with the Roxtons.

The suspense is kept going by the increasingly difficult position of the main female character, Lorna Garrett, who draws suspicion on herself by her presence in Chapman's flat, and who adds to it by her reactions and her deep suspicion of almost all her new acquaintances. This character is not so much a red herring as 'the spanner in the works' – the unforeseen element which wrecks Mrs English's plan to keep the painting. The reader is encouraged to take Lorna's side, yet there is always the possibility that she is not quite what she seems, but a decoy planted either by her aunt Mildred Garrett or Philip Dadurian.

The thrust of misdirection of the reader's attention refers back to the rivalry of the two art collectors, the prime motive of the theft of the painting from the salesroom. This provides various red herrings: Charlie Hackett and his gang, looking for the painting so that they may collect their promised fee; Joseph Marcus, whose employment of Lorna draws down Hackett on himself; Philip Dadurian, acting on his own, or in conjunction with Mildred Garrett; Irene Alderley, whose nationality (Greek) suggests she might be an agent of Panaclos, and who is used, later, to deliver a ransom note to Lorna.

The plot narrative continues:

- Mrs English searches Lorna's flat. *She wants to find out about the girl her son Brian fancies. She uses the key from Boland's handbag.*
- Lorna comes home, finds things not quite in the order in which she had left them, suspects search. Rings Freddie.
- Two of Hackett's boys force their way in and threaten Lorna, calling her Eve. *They have fallen for Freddie's lie and want to know where 'it' (the painting) is. Lorna is frightened and mystified.*
- Randall interrupts, letting himself into flat with key. *He has seen them arrive, suspects a meeting of thieves, is surprised to find one of boys brandishing a knife.* He frightens them off by announcing the police are on way.
- Freddie arrives, pretends horror, offers to fetch his assistant to stay with Lorna for a few days. Goes to fetch Simmonds.
- Randall sends for police. *He is surprised that Lorna is keen to see them. She is highly suspicious of Randall.*
- Joseph Marcus receives request to open shop after hours to oblige Dadurian. Goes to Bond Street. Hackett's boys are waiting for him, and beat him up. *Hackett thinks Marcus must be Lorna's partner and must have the painting.*
- CS Southam interviews Lorna. *She is shocked to find herself under suspicion. No one tells her why. She is highly indignant.*
- Marcus's housekeeper raises alarm. *She has phoned the shop but can get no reply. Mr Marcus is missing.*
- Southam takes Lorna to open up shop. Marcus unconscious but alive. He is taken to hospital.
- Lorna is sent home. Finds Freddie and Simmonds waiting for her in Mrs English's flat. *Simmonds is introduced to all under her nickname 'Friday', to hide her identity*

as an investigator, and to keep other interested parties occupied in putting pressure on Lorna. Simmonds and Freddie are keen to find the painting before anyone else.

- On leaving the flat, Freddie sees mirror in hall askew. Straightens it but it slips back at once. *The weight of the painting hidden in its back has put it off balance.*
- Simmonds moves in with Lorna. Freddie changes the lock on Lorna's front door. Lorna keeps two keys, gives the third to Simmonds.
- Next morning, Lorna visits Marcus in hospital. He describes his attackers. Lorna recognises them as the same two who came to her. *Marcus works out that they are after the painting and relates history of theft.*
- Southam explains to Lorna the nature of the trap he set at the flat. He wants to know how she obtained the lease. *Lorna does not know. Aunt Mildred arranged it. Southam's suspicions increase.*
- Lorna phones New York, but her aunt is away. She stays at the shop, with one of Southam's men in the office. She finds book on Flemish art with picture of missing painting. *She is surprised to discover that Randall is the author; her suspicions of him deepen. Decides to take book home and confront him.*
- Mid-afternoon, Simmonds, working in Freddie's shop, receives a phone call, purporting to come from Lorna, asking her to come back to the flat. Simmonds leaves, and finds Hackett's boys waiting for her at the flat. They take her away.
- A woman enters Marcus's shop. Tells Lorna that Hackett is holding Simmonds, not to call for help, but to be at her flat between nine-thirty and ten that evening to receive instructions. As proof, she gives Lorna a necklace. She recognises it as part of the matching set of necklace and earrings that Simmonds was wearing
- Lorna alerts police as soon as woman has gone. *She knows the ransom will be the painting, which she cannot produce.*
- Lorna goes back to the hospital to talk to Mr Marcus. She discovers that Dadurian's name was used to lure him to the shop. *She did not know he was in London, and is shocked that Marcus seems to suspect him.*
- Lorna returns to shop, pretends to work late, then,

when it is dark, slips her police guard, and goes to see Dadurian. Dadurian is shocked at the story, offers to pay Hackett the fee he lost over the painting.

- Lorna waits at home for Hackett's instructions. Southam is there. *He is highly suspicious of Dadurian's offer.*
- Hackett's woman agent is in street outside flats. She waits for a resident to appear. Mrs Alderley comes home, and is asked to deliver a letter to Lorna's door. *It is the ransom note. The random choice of her to take in the letter brings her under temporary suspicion, due to her nationality, of being an agent of Panaclos and Hackett. Enclosed with the letter is one of Simmonds's earrings.*
- Next morning, Lorna takes money to the rendezvous. *The notes are marked, so police can trace them.* It is accepted in lieu of painting.
- Lorna returns to flat. Aunt Mildred calls from New York. Reveals it was Freddie who found the flat for Lorna. Lorna goes in search of Freddie. *He has a lot of explaining to do.*
- Simmonds, released, returns to Lorna's flat, meeting Brian on the stairs. She takes off her remaining earring, leaving it in the ashtray on the coffee table. She puts on another pair. She sees the book on Flemish art. Opens it to picture of missing painting, sees fleeting likeness to Brian. *A wild idea enters her head.*
- Simmonds goes down to Brian's flat. He is not there, but his mother is. Simmonds asks a few questions. *Mrs English understands she has made the connection.*
- Mrs English offers to take Simmonds to Brian's office to question him. *Feigns great anxiety.* In garage, strangles her, takes her key to Lorna's flat, drives a mile to dump body. *Traces of body in boot. Mrs English unconcerned. Certain she will not be suspected.*
- Lorna returns home, having failed to find Freddie. He turns up, in time to hear Southam announce the finding of Simmonds's body. *Freddie distraught, lets out her real name.*
- Lorna taxes Freddie with setting her up. He admits it.

How to catch your murderer (or other villain)

The point has now been reached when it is time to draw together all the various threads and start winding up towards the dénouement, the exposure of the criminal.

A criminal who is easy to catch is not particularly interesting. A really spectacular villain can carry on for book after book without the reading public tiring of him. But in most crime stories, the criminal is an amateur, a murderer for one specific purpose, who must be caught.

Marshalling the clues

Look over your plot narrative and pick out the relevant clues. Evaluate them: do they point significantly to one character? Do they contain enough evidence to make an arrest likely? At this stage, the answer may well be 'No'. If so, as you plan the final section of the plot narrative, you must try to plan further clues and/or a mistake on the part of the murderer.

A murderer who made no mistakes would never be caught. Even if the police know he is guilty, but cannot prove it, the murderer wins.

Confessions

There are times when the writer has to fall back on the device of the murderer's confession. This is valid when the murderer has been pushed into such a position that he is trapped in his own crime – when the purpose of the killing has turned sour, and all is lost. In such circumstances, a confession can make a strong ending.

A confession can also be used when the investigation has been done by someone who has no police powers of arrest, and needs it to offer to the local constabulary. This is most likely to be used in the psychological crime novel, where the killer has been driven to crime in order to resolve an unbearable situation, or to satisfy an uncontrollable impulse for revenge.

The solution of the crime

The sequence is:

- Wind up the sub-plots, to free the red herrings of suspicion, or, if this cannot be done until the murderer is caught, make it clear that the investigator marginalises them.
- Build up to the murderer's fatal mistake, which should be bad enough to shock them either into confession or rash action.
- Plan the final explanations. The old whodunnit trick of gathering the suspects together and gradually eliminating one after another should be used with caution, if at all. To modern readers, it makes a slow ending. Ideally, the book should end on a high note.
- Keep the aftermath of the arrest as short as possible. Obviously, your characters will go on living, and their lives will be changed, one way or another. The lines of what may happen to them can be indicated before the final shock of the dénouement. If you feel obliged to take a look at them afterwards, tie up the loose ends, if any, then leave it. The party's over.

Worked example – Death Trap V(g)

Clues to murderer's identity

- Brian English resembles his grandfather, the old Duke of Roxton, who fancied himself as the model of his ancestor in the painting. It is a fleeting likeness, depending on tricks of the light. Boland saw it. So did Simmonds, later. It had completely escaped Randall (who as an art historian should have picked it up), and Southam, who has seen Brian only on odd occasions. No one at the flats, not even Mrs Fitzroy, knows of the connection with the Roxton family. Mrs English never speaks of it, having been given the cold shoulder by them all her life. Brian does not care.

- Mrs Fitzroy knows Boland was looking for Brian on the

day of her death, but it is buried in the back of her fluffy mind.

- Mrs English has keys to Lorna's flat, one from Boland's handbag, one from Simmonds's pocket.
- The weight of the painting hidden in the back of the mirror sends the frame hanging out of true. Freddie tried to put it straight and failed. So far, this means nothing to anyone.
- Simmonds lost one earring (put into the ransom note), and left the other in the flat. No one has noticed it.
- Simmonds's body is found wearing a pair of earrings. This will be recognised as a clue only when the earring is found in the flat, proving that she returned to the flat after her release.
- The only clue from the murders of the two women which is known to the police is that both were killed in the same way, by a professionally trained killer.
- There are traces of Simmonds's body in the boot of Mrs English's car. In her handbag are Lorna's keys obtained from Boland and Simmonds. In her wardrobe are Boland's handbag, and a boxful of medals and mementoes of wartime activities. Mrs English is under no suspicion, so no search of her flat or car has been considered.

Evaluation

The clues are all in place, but, as yet, there is no pointer to Mrs English as the murderer. She will not be caught unless she is tempted to further action, which will lead to a mistake or which will go wrong through factors of which she is ignorant.

Winding up sub-plots

One has already been wound up: the plot hatched by Freddie and Simmonds has been exposed. Lorna's position as an innocent party has been established.

There remain the sub-plots involving: Hackett and gang; Dadurian; Mrs Alderley; and the two men who have personal interests in Lorna, Brian English and Randall.

Worked example – Death Trap V(h)

The solution of the crime

- Dadurian admits to engaging Simmonds to investigate. *He did not know she had involved Lorna. Paid money to get both girls off the hook.*
- Brian insists that Lorna and his mother go to their country cottage until crimes cleared up. *He is deeply shocked at Simmonds's murder.* He takes Lorna down to his mother's flat to arrange for immediate departure. *Lorna not sure if she wants to be cooped up with Mrs English, but anxious to leave flat. She thinks Hackett has killed Simmonds, and will be after her.*
- Southam traces marked money back to Hackett. Arrests him.
- Mrs English is out. Brian lets himself and Lorna in with his own key. Offers to show her his mother's medals. *Attempt to reassure her.* Passing through hall, he sees the mirror askew, tried to straighten it out, takes it down to see what is wrong. Finds painting.
- Brian explains Roxton connection. *Lorna sympathetic.*
- Mrs English walks in on them. *Sees the game is up. She expects Lorna to call the police.*
- Lorna suggests the painting be returned quietly to its owners. *She has not made the connection with the murders.* Suggests Freddie would be ideal intermediary, could pretend Simmonds had left him clue to where to find the painting. *It has to wait until morning, Freddie is at the police station.*
- Lorna takes charge of painting. *To keep Mrs English's past secret, even Freddie must not know she is involved.*
- All three go to Lorna's flat. Painting is hidden under the spare-room bed. Lorna finds Simmonds's earring. *Mrs English is filled with panic, feels threatened for the first time. Knows she must eliminate Lorna.*
- Hackett, under pressure, admits was working for Panaclos. Denies all knowledge of Mrs Alderley. *Southam is left with no clues to lead him to murderer of Boland and Simmonds.*
- Brian insists on sleeping in Lorna's spare room to guard her and the painting.

93

- Next morning: Lorna goes to see Freddie to persuade him to fall in with her plan.
- Brian goes out to see client, taking Lorna's spare key.
- Mrs English shops for materials to make anti-personnel bomb which will also cause a fire. *Uses wartime training again, hoping to dispose of Lorna and let Brian think painting has been burnt.* Assembles bomb, takes it up to Lorna's flat, entering with Simmonds's key, sets it to explode when door opens.
- Randall hears someone let themselves in, then go out again. *He assumes it is Lorna, but makes no move, being consumed with rage over Brian spending the night in the flat.*
- Brian comes back, goes up to Lorna's flat, opens door, and detonates bomb. He is killed.
- Lorna returns as the body is being brought out. *Mrs English sees her and faints, realising she has killed her son.*
- She is taken into her own flat. Lorna and other residents crowd in. Lorna sees mirror hanging askew again. Tells police to look behind it. *She realises Mrs English has taken back the painting, must have planted the bomb, and by inference must have killed the two women.*
- Mrs English confesses. *She is too proud to do anything else, after all, she is a duke's daughter.*

Exercise 5

The worked example provides you with a detailed plot narrative. Using this as a pattern, write a narrative of your own plot.

7

PLANNING THE BOOK

The plot narrative sets out the entire history of the crime, from its origins to final solution. However, it is not, necessarily, the way in which the book will be written. The plot is the vehicle for the theme, which will govern the shape of the book. The plot narrative will have to be reorganised to fit that.

The synopsis

The synopsis is the scheme of work for writing the book, based upon the plot narrative. Few crimes stories will follow the plot narrative in chronological sequence. For the purpose of suspense and mystification, sections of it will have to be concealed, hinted at in clues, and fully explained only at the solution of the crime. For the purposes of the theme, other sections may have to be relegated to background information.

The synopsis can range from the vague to the highly detailed. The choice of method is personal, depending on the tastes of the writer. The extremes are:

- Vague: planning is limited to deciding where to start and knowing the position thoroughly at that point; knowing where and how it will end; introducing the action of the plot, characters, clues and red herrings in a flexible sequence, directed by natural development of the book.
- Highly detailed: everything planned – divided into chapters, containing the action to be covered, characters

introduced, red herrings and clues put into place; each chapter with a strong finishing point.

Both methods are valid. Ways of working depend on individual temperament. Some writers find it easier to hold all the various threads of the narrative in their heads; others prefer to write it all down before they begin. Many writers concoct their own methods somewhere between the two extremes.

Beginners will eventually find their own way of working. Unless they find the detailed synopsis too constricting, it is advisable for them to try working that way. The worked example at the end of this chapter shows the plot narrative divided up and annotated to form a synopsis.

The starting point

All stories are continuous. The characters enter the narrative at a certain stage in their lives, bringing their pasts along with them.

Somewhere in this continuity, a break has to be made and a place for the novel to begin chosen. This may sound obvious, but it is a serious problem. Looking at any plot narrative, various possible starting points suggest themselves. If you choose the wrong one, the narrative will not flow smoothly; the book will get bogged down; there will be no impetus to drive the words on to the page – in a word, the book will be *dull*. The only remedy is to go back to the plot narrative and find an alternative starting point.

The point at which the novel starts has to be one of high tension which will catch the reader's attention, and set the plot rolling at a good pace. Also, it should in some way announce the theme. One of the most perfect examples of this technique is to be found in the opening lines of Jane Austen's *Pride and Prejudice*: 'It is a truth universally acknowledged, that a single man in possession of a good fortune, must be in want of a wife.'

Having chosen the starting point, a line can be drawn across the plot narrative. Everything above the line is history, yet vital to make sense of the plot, and will have to be communicated to the reader in the course of writing the book. Everything below the line will form the action of the book, but some events will not appear in the text except in the form of their results – for example, the actions of the murderer, concealed for the purpose of maintaining suspense.

Any characters who appear in the section above the line, but who have no active part below the line, can be relegated to 'mention only' status in the book itself. Any reduction in the number of characters the reader has to cope with is an advantage. Minor characters, in particular, can proliferate, and should be kept to a minimum.

Developing the theme

The plot narrative is concerned with the progress of the crime and its aftermath. It is the framework on to which the theme is grafted. A stark narration of the history of a crime would not make fascinating reading. It is the effect upon human beings, and particularly on the main characters and the problems with which they struggle, that can involve the reader, encouraging him to identify with at least one of the protagonists and to take an interest in what happens to them.

The development of the theme is accomplished through the main characters. Their relationship to each other and to the other characters, the conflict which arises and its resolution, provide a thread to be woven into the action of the plot to bring it to life.

All this has to be worked into the synopsis, along with, and arising from, the stages of unrolling the plot. Some human reactions are already built into the plot narrative. Those reactions necessary for the development of the theme – arguments, quarrels, suspicions, misunderstandings, efforts to protect others, and so on – have to be added to the synopsis to provide a steady progression of the theme throughout the book.

The viewpoint

At this stage, it is necessary to decide from whose angle the story is to be told. This makes a material difference to the synopsis.

Where the theme does not give a firm indication of the viewpoint, the choices are:

- A first-person narrative. There is the limitation that nothing can be recorded except what that particular character sees, feels, hears, and experiences. The thoughts and attitudes of other characters are seen only through their actions as viewed by the narrator.
- A third-person narrative but with a single viewpoint. This is virtually the same as a first-person narrative, but more flexible. Without making the stylistic error of occasionally switching to the viewpoint of another character, the reader can be made aware of what goes on behind the main character's back and appreciate the importance of things which do not, as yet, mean anything to the character.
- A multi-viewpoint narrative. Here the viewpoint can shift from one character to another. This is useful where the writer wishes to keep several lines of action going at once. Each chapter will have sections showing what is happening simultaneously or in close succession in a given period of time.
- If the main feature of the novel is to be a police investigation, with action shown and characters introduced in advance of the detective's arrival, a multiple viewpoint has to be used. In this case, care should be taken that the initial characters are not 'dropped' once the investigation is in progress.

Introducing the characters

Since the theme is developed through the actions of the main characters, they should be introduced as early as possible in the narrative, at least in the first chapter if not actually on the opening page. It is important to fix them in the reader's mind as the principals.

Characters should be introduced one by one. At the beginning of a book, the reader may become confused, wondering who is who. Slow and steady introduction of the characters gives time for each one to sink into the mind of the reader.

The starting point might be, for instance, at a party, where perhaps as many as four or five characters can be introduced in rapid succession. If it is unavoidable, scatter the characters about the place. A party implies the presence of a number of people who can be spread out over a fair amount of space. Suppose the setting to be a nightclub. Having all the characters seated round one table would be difficult to handle. For the purposes of introduction, split them up – they can be dancing, or in the cloakroom, or out on the terrace, or at the bar – so that the reader may view them separately before they all come together in one place.

Introducing a whole group of characters all in one go is never easy. It is best avoided, and should not be tackled by a beginner. Organise the synopsis so that the characters are fed in smoothly, and the readers will take them in their stride.

Dealing with background information

The choice of the starting point relegates a certain amount of information relevant to the crime to the position of background material. The problem arises of how to work this into the synopsis.

In my view, the least desirable device to use is that of flashback. The only thing that can be said for flashback is that it is easy. However, it stops the action dead in its tracks; and dodging around time confuses the reader. Flashback is an extended form of a long, dreary description. Readers often skip those, and they may do the same to a flashback. This defeats its purpose, which is to convey necessary information.

Other ways of introducing background material have to be found:

- Feed it to the readers in snippets, through conversations and discoveries.
- Use some form of prologue. If the content is interesting enough, this can be a device for hooking the reader.
- If the plot permits, and the amount of background material is too great to be conveyed by either of the above methods, the book may be divided into parts, each a complete entity, but linked by the theme.

'Off-stage' action, which goes on simultaneously with the main run of the plot but which cannot be shown, has to be communicated to the reader through the words of other characters, the finding of a body or the planting of clues which will not be appreciated until further on in the plot. This includes steps taken by the murderer to divert suspicion, and sideshows staged by other characters pursuing their own ends. These things have to be indicated at the appropriate places on the synopsis.

Clues and red herrings

All clues leading to the solution of the crime must be indicated in the synopsis, as must false trails leading to suspicion falling on those characters scheduled as red herrings.

Endings

The plot will have provided the solution to the crime, but that does not necessarily imply that the theme has also been wound up. The conflicts of the theme have to be resolved in some way to make a satisfactory ending.

The ending does not have to be a happy one. It needs to be one which is logical in the light of the action all through the book, and which leaves the reader with a feeling of satisfaction. Loose ends should be tidied up, obscurities clarified. There are few things more irritating to a reader than being left wondering exactly what happened.

The temptation is to spend time seeing the main characters on their way into a continuation of life; certainly they cannot be left suspended in mid-air. Some indication of what is likely to happen to them should be given but, whatever this may be, it should be kept brief.

Dividing the synopsis into chapters

With all this work done, there remains one final task before the synopsis is ready. This is the division of the material into chapters.

A book written in one continuous narrative without divisions would be difficult both to write and to read. Each chapter should relate what happens at successive stages of the plot, develop a bit of the theme, and hold its quota of clues and pieces of information about backgrounds to the crime and the characters.

There needs to be a balance in the action, so that the reader can keep track of the various threads in the story and stay abreast of its character. Characters who have dropped out of the action for a period can be kept alive in the reader's mind through references made to what they are doing, or through other characters' puzzlement if they seem to have vanished.

The aim of each chapter is to forward the action to a certain point. Chapters form convenient divisions of the story. For the writer they help to give form to the book; to the reader, they provide a goal. He can decide to read as far as, say, the end of the chapter, then lay the book aside; few people read a book at a sitting.

Crime writers aim to make the narrative so gripping that the readers cannot bring themselves to put the book down. The device to tempt them to read on, from chapter to chapter, is the cliffhanger.

The name derives from the 1920s, when the pulp magazines burst upon the world with serials where the hero or heroine was left in some terrible situation – perhaps literally hanging off a cliff by their fingers. The outcome would not be known until the next instalment was published.

In the context of a novel, the use of the cliffhanger comes at the end of each chapter, leaving a situation so intriguing that the reader is impelled to read on. Once the trick has worked, the reader has become a captive, and will be stuck to the book for as long as it takes to read it.

When dividing the synopsis into chapters, look for the moments when something exciting is happening and divide the action into two, so that one half is a chapter ending, and the other the beginning of the next.

This brings the synopsis to completion. All is now ready to begin writing the book.

Worked example – Death Trap VI

Starting point

The starting point has to be at the entry of the main female character, Lorna. This means that a great deal of the history of the crime has taken place before the story opens.

Developing the theme: self-development

Lorna starts from a position of ignorance of the facts of her situation. Her trip to England is very exciting, opening up another world to her. The latent strength of her character appears, firstly, in her indignation when she senses deep suspicion of her from both Randall and CS Southam; and, secondly, in her resolve to fight her way out of the trap once she understands how she is being used as bait. But her judgement is unformed, and she consistently chooses the wrong people to suspect and to trust.

To develop this theme through the action of the plot, certain ideas suggest themselves:

- Randall will stick to her like glue, and will figure in many of the scenes.
- Randall and Lorna will spend a good deal of their time quarrelling.
- Freddie will be prominent, playing his part as a false

friend and fuelling Lorna's suspicions of Randall for his own purposes.

- Lorna will have constant brushes with CS Southam. She is resentful of his suspicions of her, and will bring further suspicion on herself by pursuing her own line of inquiry.
- Lorna will put personal loyalties first, protecting Dadurian out of long-standing affection, and Mrs English out of respect for Brian.

Viewpoint

The theme indicates that this story will be told from Lorna's viewpoint, either as a first-person narrative or a third-person concentrated upon the girl.

Introducing the characters

The order of introduction must be: Lorna, Randall, Freddie, Southam. The action revolves mainly round these four, with minor characters appearing from time to time. The murderer, Mrs English, is deliberately kept on the sidelines, though she makes herself well known through the force of her character.

Background information

The history of the crime will be revealed largely through Lorna's efforts to find out why everyone seems to suspect her.

Ending

The solution, also, will come about largely through Lorna's activities, which result in the finding of the painting; but even then she fails to understand the implications of her discovery and where guilt for two murders has to lie. That failure leads to the final tragedy.

In its original form, *Death Trap* had a happy ending for

Lorna and Randall. If I were writing it today, I doubt if I would give it such a definite ending. I think it would be more logical to leave it with the two main characters aware of a bond between them created by the shared experience, and only hint at a possible shared life at some time in the future.

The synopsis:

BACKGROUND MATERIAL

- Duke of Roxton decides to send painting to auction to pay death duties (MENTION ONLY). Estimated price £750,000. *Mrs English is horrified. Was her father's favourite picture. Wonders if she could raise enough to buy it. Dadurian and Panaclos both want it.*
- Panaclos engages Hackett to steal painting before sale, for fee of £250,000 (MENTION ONLY). *Hackett puts pressure on Chapman (partner in salesroom)* (MENTION ONLY), *holds IOU for large gambling debt. Chapman yields to pressure to clear debt.*
- Theft carried out on view-day. Painting taken out in briefcase. Chapman goes home to phone Hackett. Omits to shut front door, expecting to go straight out again. *A porter notices Chapman's briefcase looks fatter than usual* (MENTION ONLY).
- Mrs English follows Chapman up to flat. *She has been to the view-day, discovers Chapman works at salesroom, hears him come home, goes up to ask him how much the painting is likely to fetch.*
- Mrs English sees painting in open briefcase on hall table, takes it, slips back downstairs. Conceals it behind mirror in her own hall (CLUE TO USE LATER). *Motive: to save it from the thief; keeps it to punish family.*
- Hackett does not believe Chapman's story, seizes him, tries torture to get truth out of him. Chapman dies of heart attack. Body dumped. *Chapman has no idea who can have stolen it. No one at flats knows of Mrs English's connection with the Roxtons* (CLUE TO USE LATER).
- CS Southam opens police inquiry. Comes up with no leads. Search of flat yields no clues. *Evidence from sales-*

room points to Chapman as thief. Body found, shows traces of torture.

- Time lag one month.
- Insurance company plants investigator, Penelope Boland, in Chapman's flat (MENTION ONLY). *Boland is playing a hunch that Chapman had one of his neighbours as an accomplice.*
- Brian English comes home for weekend. Boland sees him. *Boland spots Brian English's likeness to Roxtons* (CLUE TO USE LATER).
- Boland makes discreet inquiries about Brian. *She picks on Mrs Fitzroy as most likely to gossip. She suspects Brian was Chapman's accomplice.*
- Mrs Fitzroy mentions this to Mrs English (CLUE TO USE LATER). *Immediately, Mrs English understands the danger.*
- Mrs English watches Boland, follows her when she goes out in evening (dark) to postbox in alley. Strangles her. *During war, she learnt killing techniques, and that survival depends on bold action when threatened* (BACKGROUND MATERIAL).
- Body left in alley. *Attempt to make it look like a mugging.*
- Mrs English takes handbag (contains key to flat). Hides it in her wardrobe (EVIDENCE).
- Southam investigates murder. *Only one clue: killing an expert job* (MRS ENGLISH'S WARTIME TRAINING). *Southam concludes Boland had got on track of painting. Clue to whereabouts must be in flat.*
- By arrangement with Chapman's executors, Southam sets a trap, circulating the rumour in Fine Arts circles that the flat is to let. He waits to see who takes it.
- Dadurian commissions a freelance investigator, Eve Simmonds, to take over Boland's task. *Simmonds eager to collect reward for finding painting as well as fee.*
- Simmonds invites antique dealer, Freddie Templeton, to work with her and share reward. *Freddie keen. She does not tell him of her connection with Dadurian.*
- Freddie remembers American friend, Mildred Garrett, has asked him to find a flat for her niece, Lorna (MENTION ONLY). He and Simmonds concoct a plan to use

Lorna as a means of getting into Chapman's flat to search it. He obtains the lease of the flat for Lorna.

- Lorna Garrett arrives from New York to work as a trainee for six months with antique dealer Joseph Marcus. She moves into the flat. *Freddie befriends her; other residents welcome her; Brian English falls for Lorna. No one tells her about the deaths of Chapman and Boland, or about the loss of the painting.*

- Freddie puts out a rumour that the new tenant of Chapman's flat is a girl called Eve, who knows where the painting is. *Lorna is being set up, to receive unwelcome attention from interested parties which will frighten her into accepting Simmonds as a live-in companion. Simmonds insists on using her own name (Eve) so that Dadurian will assume she is the actual tenant, and will make sure his own people will leave her alone. Freddie is willing to go along with anything she says. Simmonds is unaware of Dadurian's connection with Lorna, as is Freddie* (IDENTITY OF EVE TO BE KEPT HIDDEN FROM READER UNTIL FREDDIE LETS OUT THE TRUTH).

- Insurance company engages Randall to watch Lorna. He is given a key to the flat to search it when the opportunity arises. *Randall fancies himself as a detective, having helped a few times. He assumes Lorna is working for someone looking for the painting* (BACKGROUND MATERIAL TO BE WORKED IN GRADUALLY).

- Hackett picks up the rumour about the new tenant. *He assumes she has taken the flat to pick up a clue left for her by Chapman to retrieve the painting from the place where he hid it. Has her watched.*

- CS Southam puts a tail on Lorna. *He thinks he has found Chapman's accomplice, who has come to retrieve the painting and hand it on to the final customer. He regards her innocent routine as mere caution. He is willing to play a waiting game.*

- Mrs English searches Lorna's flat. *She wants to find out about the girl her son Brian fancies. She uses the key from Boland's handbag* (BACKGROUND MATERIAL ENDS HERE).

NOVEL OPENS HERE
CHAPTER ONE

- Lorna comes home, finds things not quite in the order in which she had left them, suspects search. Rings Freddie. Two of Hackett's boys force their way in and threaten Lorna, calling her Eve. *They have fallen for Freddie's lie and want to know where 'it' (the painting) is. Lorna is frightened and mystified.*
- Randall interrupts, letting himself into flat with key. *He has seen them arrive, suspects a meeting of thieves, is surprised to find one of boys brandishing a knife.* He frightens them off by announcing the police are on way. (RANDALL A PEST. LORNA GLAD OF HIS RESCUE UNTIL BEGINS TO THINK IT WAS TOO PAT. SUSPECTS HE HAS KEY. HOW DID HE GET IT?)
- Freddie arrives, pretends horror, offers to fetch his assistant to stay with Lorna for a few days. (FREDDIE TRIES TO THROW SUSPICION ON RANDALL.) Goes to fetch Simmonds.

END CHAPTER ON SUDDEN CRISIS OF SUSPICION OF RANDALL.

CHAPTER TWO

- Randall sends for police. *He is surprised that Lorna is keen to see them. She is highly suspicious of Randall.* (LORNA ANGRY WHEN FINDS HE SUSPECTS HER.)
- Joseph Marcus receives request to open shop after hours to oblige Dadurian. Goes to Bond Street. Hackett's boys are waiting for him, and beat him up. *Hackett thinks Marcus must be Lorna's partner and has the painting.* (DELETE FROM ACTION. STORY BY MARCUS WHEN REGAINS CONSCIOUSNESS.)
- CS Southam interviews Lorna. *She is shocked to find herself under suspicion. No one tells her why. She is highly indignant.* (LORNA SUSPECTS SOUTHAM TRYING TO TRAP HER. NOT PLEASED TO FIND RANDALL SEEMS TO HAVE SOME STANDING WITH POLICE.)

- Marcus's housekeeper raises alarm. *She has phoned the shop but can get no reply. Mr Marcus is missing.*
- Southam takes Lorna to open up shop. Marcus unconscious but alive. He is taken to hospital.

END CHAPTER ON DISCOVERY OF MARCUS.

CHAPTER THREE

- Lorna is sent home. Finds Freddie and Simmonds waiting for her in Mrs English's flat. *Simmonds is introduced to all under her nickname 'Friday', to hide her identity as an investigator, and to keep other interested parties occupied in putting pressure on Lorna. Simmonds and Freddie are keen to find the painting before anyone else.* (LORNA IS STARTING TO RELY ON FREDDIE. SHE ACCEPTS SIMMONDS AS A FRIEND. IS IMPRESSED BY HER GLAMOUR. FREDDIE SUGGESTS RANDALL IS IN WITH WHOEVER SENT THUGS.)
- On leaving the flat, Freddie sees mirror in hall askew. Straightens it but it slips back at once. *The weight of the painting hidden in its back has put it off balance.*
- Simmonds moves in with Lorna. Freddie changes the lock on Lorna's front door. Lorna keeps two keys, gives the third to Simmonds.

END CHAPTER ON LORNA'S INCREASING DISTRUST OF RANDALL.

CHAPTER FOUR

- Next morning, Lorna visits Marcus in hospital. He describes his attackers. Lorna recognises them as the same two who came to her. *Marcus works out that they are after the painting and relates history of theft.*
- Southam explains to Lorna the nature of the trap he set at the flat. He wants to know how she obtained the lease. *Lorna does not know. Aunt Mildred arranged it. Southam's suspicions increase.*
- Lorna phones New York, but her aunt is away. She stays at the shop, with one of Southam's men in the office. She finds book on Flemish art with picture of the missing painting. *She is surprised to discover that Randall*

is the author, suspicions of him deepen. Decides to take book home and confront him. (LORNA UNDER POLICE GUARD. TO HER DISCOMFORT RANDALL TAGS ALONG. AFTER HOSPITAL VISIT HE GOES WITH HER TO SHOP, PUMPS HER ON BACKGROUND. RANDALL TURNS HOSTILE, THINKS SHE PRETENDS IGNORANCE OF PAINTING BEFORE MARCUS'S TALE. THEY QUARREL.)

- Mid-afternoon Simmonds, working in Freddie's shop, receives a phone call, purporting to come from Lorna, asking her to come back to the flat. Simmonds leaves, finds Hackett's boys waiting for her. They take her away. (DELETE FROM ACTION. BACKGROUND ONLY.)

- (LORNA ALONE IN SHOP. POLICE GUARD IN OFFICE AT BACK.) A woman enters Marcus's shop, and tells Lorna that Hackett is holding Simmonds, Lorna is not to call for help, but is to be at her flat between nine-thirty and ten that evening to receive instructions. As proof, the woman gives Lorna a necklace. She recognises it as part of the matching set of necklace and earrings that Simmonds was wearing.

END CHAPTER HERE.

CHAPTER FIVE

- Lorna alerts police as soon as woman has gone. *She knows the ransom will be the painting, which she cannot produce.*

- Lorna goes back to the hospital to talk to Mr Marcus. She discovers that Dadurian's name was used to lure him to the shop. *She did not know he was in London, and is shocked that Marcus seems to suspect him.* (FIRST HINT OF SUSPICION OF DADURIAN. EXPLAIN LORNA'S RELATIONSHIP TO HIM.)

- Lorna returns to shop, pretends to work late, then, when it is dark, slips her police guard, and goes to see Dadurian. (GUARD IS IN CAR AT DOOR OF SHOP. LORNA USES BACK WAY.) Dadurian is shocked at the story, offers to pay Hackett the fee he lost over the painting.

END CHAPTER ON RANDALL CATCHING LORNA ON RETURN.

CHAPTER SIX

- Lorna waits at home for Hackett's instructions. Southam is there. *He is highly suspicious of Dadurian's offer.* (RANDALL MORE FRIENDLY. WHY? LORNA SUSPICIOUS. BRIAN COMES HOME, GETS LORNA TO HIMSELF AND TELLS OF MRS ENGLISH'S WAR SERVICE. RANDALL THINKS SHE HAS BEEN OFF AGAIN ALONE.)
- Hackett's woman agent is in street outside flats. She waits for a resident to appear. Mrs Alderley comes home, and is asked to deliver a letter to Lorna's door. *It is the ransom note. The random choice of her to take in the letter brings her under temporary suspicion, due to her nationality, of being an agent of Panaclos and Hackett. Enclosed with the letter is one of Simmonds's earrings.*

END CHAPTER ON QUARREL BETWEEN RANDALL AND LORNA.

CHAPTER SEVEN

- Next morning, Lorna takes money to rendezvous. *The notes are marked, so police can trace them.* It is accepted in lieu of painting. (LORNA NOW SURE RANDALL WAS CHAPMAN'S ACCOMPLICE. RANDALL ADMITS HE HAS KEY. HE TELLS HER ABOUT BOLAND. THEY QUARREL.)
- Lorna returns to flat. Aunt Mildred calls from New York. Reveals it was Freddie who found the flat for Lorna. Lorna goes in search of Freddie, *He has a lot of explaining to do.*
- Simmonds, released, returns to Lorna's flat, meeting Brian on the stairs. She takes off her remaining earring, leaving it in the ashtray on the coffee-table (CLUE). She puts on another pair. She sees the book on Flemish art and opens it to picture of missing painting. She sees a fleeting likeness to Brian. *A wild idea enters her head.*
- Simmonds goes down to Brian's flat. He is not there,

but his mother is. Simmonds asks a few questions. *Mrs English understands she has made the connection.* (DELETE FROM ACTION. BACKGROUND ONLY.)

- Mrs English offers to take Simmonds to Brian's office to question him. *Feigns great anxiety.* In garage, strangles her, takes her key (EVIDENCE TO FIND LATER) to Lorna's flat, drives a mile to dump body. *Traces of body in boot* (EVIDENCE TO BE FOUND LATER). *Mrs English unconcerned. Sure will not be suspected.*
- Lorna returns home, having failed to find Freddie. He turns up, in time to hear Southam announce the finding of Simmonds's body (CLUE: *PAIR* OF EARRINGS). *Freddie distraught, lets out her real name.*

END CHAPTER HERE

CHAPTER EIGHT

- Lorna taxes Freddie with setting her up. He admits it.
- Dadurian admits to engaging Simmonds to investigate. *He did not know she had involved Lorna. Paid money to get both girls off the hook.* (RANDALL SUSPECTS LORNA IS IN A PLOT WITH DADURIAN. THEY HAVE A FRESH QUARREL; THEIR ANTAGONISM IS DUE TO MUTUAL ATTRACTION WHICH BOTH RESIST.)
- Brian insists that Lorna and his mother go to their country cottage until crimes cleared up. *He is deeply shocked at Simmonds's murder.* He takes Lorna down to his mother's flat to arrange for immediate departure. (LORNA IS WILLING TO GO TO SPITE RANDALL.) *Lorna not sure if she wants to be cooped up with Mrs English, but anxious to leave flat. She thinks Hackett has killed Simmonds, and will be after her.*
- Southam traces marked money back to Hackett. Arrests him. (DELETE FROM ACTION. BACKGROUND ONLY.)
- Mrs English is out. Brian lets himself and Lorna in with his own key. Offers to show her his mother's medals. *Attempt to reassure her.* Passing through hall, he sees mirror askew, tries to straighten it, takes it down to see what is wrong. Find painting.

111

END CHAPTER ON THIS DISCOVERY.

CHAPTER NINE

- Brian explains Roxton connection. *Lorna sympathetic.*
- Mrs English walks in on them. *Sees the game is up. She expects Lorna to call the police.*
- Lorna suggests the painting be returned to its owners quietly. *She has not made the connection with the murders.* Suggests Freddie would be ideal intermediary, could pretend Simmons had left him clue to where to find the painting. Being allowed to collect the reward would persuade him. *It has to wait until morning, Freddie is at the police station.* (MRS ENGLISH APPARENTLY GLAD OF CHANCE TO RETURN PAINTING AND GRATEFUL POLICE NOT CALLED. THIS IS NOT THE CASE.)
- Lorna takes charge of painting. *To keep Mrs English's part secret, even Freddie must not know she is involved.*
- All three go to Lorna's flat. Painting is hidden under the spare-room bed. Lorna finds Simmonds's earring. *Mrs English is filled with panic, and feels threatened for the first time. Know she must eliminate Lorna.*
- Hackett, under pressure, admits was working for Panaclos. Denies all knowledge of Mrs Alderley. *Southam is left with no clues to lead him to murderer of Boland and Simmonds.* (MENTION THIS LATER TO CLEAR MRS ALDERLEY.)
- Brian insists on sleeping in Lorna's spare room to guard her and the painting. (RANDALL SEES HIM LEAVE IN THE MORNING AND IS VERY ANGRY, THINKING THE WORST.)
- Next morning: Lorna goes to see Freddie to persuade him to fall in with her plan. (LORNA OUT A LONG TIME.)
- Brian goes out to see client, taking Lorna's spare key.
- Mrs. English shops for materials to make anti-personnel bomb which will cause a fire also. *Using wartime training again, hoping to dispose of Lorna and let Brian think painting has been burnt.* Assembles it, takes it up to Lorna's flat, entering with Simmonds's key, sets it to explode when door opens. (NOT SHOWN IN

ACTION. BACKGROUND TO BE USED IN EVIDENCE LATER.)

- Randall hears someone let themselves in, then go out again. *He assumes it is Lorna, but makes no move, being consumed with rage over Brian spending the night in the flat.*
- Brian comes back, goes up to Lorna's flat, opens door, and detonates bomb. He is killed. (LORNA IS THE INTENDED VICTIM. RANDALL THINKS SHE IS DEAD UNTIL BRIAN IS BROUGHT OUT.)
- Lorna returns as the body is being brought out. *Mrs English sees her and faints, realising she had killed her son.*

END CHAPTER HERE.

CHAPTER TEN

- She is taken into her own flat. Lorna and the other residents crowd in. Lorna sees mirror hanging askew again. Tells police to look behind it. *She realises Mrs English has taken back the painting, must have planted the bomb, and by inference must have killed the two women.* (BEGIN TO TIE UP LOOSE ENDS. THE BOMB BRINGS CHARACTERS AND POLICE ALL TOGETHER.)
- Mrs English confesses. *She is too proud to do anything else, after all, she is a duke's daughter.*
- Ending – resolve situation between Lorna and Randall.

Exercise 6

Take your plot narrative and, following the pattern of the worked example, make out a synopsis.

8

WRITING THE BOOK

All the preparatory work has been done, and the synopsis is ready. The time has arrived to get down to the business of writing the book. As a physical task, it is demanding. A great deal of effort is required to produce a typescript of 60,000 words or more, no matter what mechanical aid is to hand. A blank page with nothing but 'Page 1, Chapter 1' at the top is a daunting sight, and the sheer number of words waiting to be written can seem depressing. Such thoughts have to be put aside and a start made.

Style

The basis of good writing is knowledge of language. All craftsmen have tools, and need to learn how to use them and how to keep them in good condition.

Language is the writer's tool. To use it, you must have a grounding in syntax and punctuation, and a wide vocabulary. Keeping the tool in good condition is a matter of practice in using words to convey your ideas, learning by trial and error what is readable and what is not, and the ruthless application of cutting.

The need to cut

All fledgling writers are so happy to find that they have the ability to string words together that they wallow in it. The result is a terrifying prolixity. The first thing is to learn how to cut, to shape the prose so that the words form a pattern that is a pleasure to read. Good writing is pared to the bone and polished so that exactly the right word is used.

Developing a style

Every writer develops their own style, suitable to the sort of book they write. Essentially, this has to be a personal style of writing, not a copy of someone else's style. Write as the words come naturally to you.

Try to develop a simple, clear style: keep sentences short; and never use a long word where a short one will do.

Repetition of words

The too-frequent use of a word makes prose boring. A well-worn but still useful tip is not to use a word more than once in any five lines. Obviously, this does not refer to the ands-and-buts, nor to the parts of verbs which form the structure of a sentence, but to nouns, adjectives, and descriptive verbs. For example: 'There was nothing we could do. The entrance was blocked. No way in, and, for us, no way out, until the entrance was cleared.'

The repetition of the word 'entrance' jars. There is no good reason why the word should be used twice. 'Gateway', 'passage' or 'exit' would fit in equally well, and would not disturb the flow of the prose.

However, repetition of a word or phrase can be used to create dramatic effect. For example: 'It was a pretty little lane, with a pretty little house at the end of it, which should have been full of pretty little people.'

Here the repetition is used deliberately to build up to a climax, almost certainly nasty, with something in the house which is distinctly neither pretty nor little.

Page layout

There is a visual aspect to style. This may sound ridiculous, but consider your own reaction to seeing a page of uninter-rupted prose, without a single break in it. If you are wrapped up in the story, you may take it in your stride. If you are not completely hooked, you may skip it, or lay the book aside until you feel you have time to tackle the monstrous lump, or even be so put off that you abandon the book. Just as a writer may be daunted by the sight of a first page with not a word yet written, so the reader may find a page crammed with words a deterrent.

A page where the text is varied is much more attractive to the eye. Breaks in the text lead the reader's eye on down the page, fostering interest in the story.

Paragraphs should be kept as short as possible. The body of information to be communicated can be broken up, to be inserted in a series of short paragraphs interspersed between pieces of dialogue or action.

Breaking up the text by giving sentences of particular dramatic interest a line to themselves can also draw the reader's interest. For example, compare two ways of writing this passage. The content is the same in both. One is written as a continuous paragraph; the other is broken up for emphasis.

I settled my back against a tree and waited. The night was utterly silent, until my ears grew used to it. Then I began to hear the soft movements of small animals, and the faint rustle of perching birds competing for a little extra room on an overcrowded branch. I listened for other sounds and heard nothing. An owl startled me, brushing past barely above my head, on slow-flapping wings. Involuntarily, I ducked. A bullet buried itself in the tree trunk with a soft plop. There had been no warning, no give-away crack of a rifle. He was out there, my enemy, with night-sights and a silencer. He knew where I was standing, to a millimetre. He would have had me, but for Brother Owl.

Now try this:

I settled my back against a tree trunk and waited.

The night was utterly silent, until my ears grew used to it. Then I began to hear the soft movements of small animals, and the faint rustle of perching birds competing for a little extra room on an overcrowded branch.

I listened for other sounds and heard nothing.

An owl startled me, brushing past barely above my head, on slow-flapping wings. Involuntarily, I ducked.

A bullet buried itself in the tree trunk with a soft plop.

There had been no warning, no give-away crack of a rifle. He was out there, my enemy, with night-sights and a silencer. He knew where I was standing, to a millimetre.

He would have had me, but for Brother Owl.

The contrast is self-evident. The second version is easier to read, and more exciting. Suspense is built up by the single sentences standing on their own, describing the listening, the shot, and the grim conclusion drawn from it. Even the most casual reader will catch these points.

Finding stylistic faults

The only way of finding stylistic, and other, faults is to check the typescript at frequent intervals. Anything that jars, no matter how small, must be dealt with.

The main problem in checking your work is the interference of your memory. You know what you meant to write, and memory will insist that that is what you put down. It may not be so. It is fatally easy to use the wrong word, or put the right word in the wrong place, and so change the meaning of the sentence.

The sure-fire way of checking your work is to put it to the test of being read aloud. Reading aloud produces a surprising effect. The ear detects faults that the eye misses. Anything badly phrased, pedantic, pompous or repetitious is spotted instantly.

Rewriting

In my experience, no first draft of a book comes through unscathed to publication. On the contrary, most books are written two or three times, or maybe more. This is because there is always a better way of doing it, as one discovers on rereading early work. Be prepared to rewrite until you are entirely satisfied.

Making a start

Nowhere is good writing more important than on the first pages of a novel. This is the place where the reader is caught – in the opening sentence, or paragraph. If readers are not hooked by the bottom of the page, the chances of holding on to them are slim.

The quality of the opening must be such that the reader's full attention will be grabbed, the mind alerted to the enticing prospect of suspense, intrigue, danger or mystery. This instant response creates a bond between writer and reader which needs to be maintained to the final page. If it is not, the readers feel let down.

Worked example – Death Trap VII(a)

Someone had been in. There was no question about it. The signs were unmistakable. The place had been searched. A careful intruder, but not quite careful enough. Things were almost as she had left them this morning.

Almost. Yet displaced enough to warn her that someone had entered her flat in her absence, and examined her possessions . . .

The thought of a stranger pawing through her things made Lorna Garrett shudder.

But this did not look like the work of a burglar. There was no disorder. Everything had been put back in place. Anyone less meticulous might never have noticed.

Almost, she wished that she had not.

Pace

The good start has to be followed up. In writing a crime novel, it is essential to remember that the pace must be maintained throughout the book. Pace is the most important factor in holding the attention of the reader. It can be sacrificed to nothing.

By its very name, crime writing is supposed to be exciting. In practice, pace is dictated by the type of story. Crime novels range from those that gallop along at breakneck speed, to slow, deep, fascinating probes into the psychology of murder. There is a readership for both these extremes, but most readers are somewhere in between, and will read a wide selection of crime novels of all types.

For the beginner, it is advisable to aim for this middle ground. Get the story going at a pace which will foster the wish to go on reading. The momentum created by the opening can be maintained by good, crisp, disciplined writing, with no sagging, no padding, no wandering off the point.

Keeping the interest going

The first chapter is written, and now is the testing time to see if the synopsis is workable. Chapter 2 can be difficult: the story has only just started; the theme is still in its infancy; characters are still to be introduced.

This is the place where the narrative may sag a little. It may be a stage in the plot where the corpse has not yet been discovered, or the police are in the throes of starting the investigation. In real life, this is a quiet period with nothing much happening. In fiction, it has to be filled with something.

This pause is the opportunity to start developing the theme. The foundations laid in Chapter 1 have to be built on immediately, so that the theme does not get swamped in the details of the crime.

The theme and the course of the crime have to be developed in parallel, until the ending, when the crime is over and only the theme remains to be resolved. This is the right order: the plot, no matter how exciting, is only the vehicle for the development of the theme.

In this early stage of the novel, most of the characters will not have awoken to the nature of their situation. They will still be pursuing their own interests, and regard the crime, or the circumstances leading up to it, as of no particular concern of theirs. This is the moment to give them intimations of the trouble about to overwhelm them; or to heighten the tension if they are already aware that all is not well in their little world.

The early stages of the story provide excellent cover for clues, particularly if the crime has not yet been committed.

Cliffhangers

It is as well to cultivate the habit of ending every chapter on an up-beat, so that the reader does not have a sense of having come to the end of something, but is encouraged to read on. Ideally, there should be a cliffhanger at the end of each chapter except, of course, the final one.

The synopsis shows where the piece of action at the end of one chapter is divided between that and the opening of the next.

Worked example – Death Trap VII(b)

The situation: Marcus is missing. He is not at home, nor with friends, nor at his club, nor admitted to hospital. There is only one place left to look, unlikely as that is this late at night: the shop. Lorna goes with the police to open it up. Bond Street at night is a bit spooky.

Mr Marcus's shop was as silent at the rest. Peering into the gloom as she unlocked the door with suddenly trembling fingers, Lorna could make out the shapes of objects familiar enough in daytime, now unreal, unknown. Light from the street fell on the upraised arms of an alabaster saint, transforming it into a semblance of life. Behind her, she heard Chief Superintendent Southam hiss with impatience at her fumbling with the lock. Then the door gave under her fingers, and she stepped across the threshold.

'Lights, Miss, please,' Southam growled, and Lorna picked her way across the shop to the switches.

And then it was all normal again, a long elegant room full of objects she dusted every day, and the alabaster saint was turned back into stone.

There was no sign of disturbance.

'The office is at the back,' Lorna said, as they stood hesitating.

That was in darkness, too. Lorna snapped on the light.

The mystery of Mr Marcus was solved. He was here, lying on the floor, with his head in a pool of blood.

That is the end of Chapter 2, leaving the reader with no idea if the man is alive or dead. Here is the opening of Chapter 3:

'Is he dead?' Lorna demanded, fearfully.

Southam was kneeling beside the still form of Mr Marcus. He looked up. 'No, not yet. He's been beaten.' Gently, he touched the old man's cheek. There was a deep gash down the side of his face. 'That was done with a knife.'

Lorna felt herself begin to shake. Once more, she could feel the nearness of the sharp blade to her own skin.

This is an easy cliffhanger: a body on the floor in a pool of blood. It is the simple wish to know if the victim is dead or alive which drives the reader to start on the next chapter. It illustrates the whole point of the device: the arousal of intense curiosity in the reader.

The example also shows part of the lead-up to the cliffhanger. The reader is expecting to find something at the shop. Tension is shown in the nervousness of Lorna, who has had a dreadful evening, being threatened by a thug with a knife; and in the impatience of Southam.

Writing the scenes

A novel is a sequence of scenes. Before writing each, certain points have to be considered:

- The point of view from which the scene is written. This arises only where multiple viewpoints are used. Try to keep to one only in each scene. Some writers regard this as a hard and fast rule. In my view, there can be exceptions, but it is better to stick to the rule as far as possible. If a change in viewpoint is necessary, keep the character for the remainder of the scene.
- Keeping to the viewpoint of only one character means that the thoughts of other characters will be expressed in concrete form of actions and speech.
- Beware of a pitfall: once embarked on revealing the private thoughts of characters, the device may be overused, disclosing material that could be brought out in speech or action – a much livelier way of doing it.

Writing in the characters

In the synopsis, the order of introduction of the characters has been worked out to avoid, as far as possible, bunching. With the appearance of each character, the aim is not to give a potted biography, but a *first impression*, exactly as if one were meeting a stranger. The description needs to be short and vivid. It will describe only the physical appearance, and the aura of cheerfulness, pleasantness, gloom or acidity which strikes those who meet this character. For the first impression, there is no room to go into details of past history or to delve into personality. Those aspects must be added, gradually, as the reader becomes more familiar with the character.

What is needed is a swift, illuminating phrase. For example: 'He was like a sparrow; neat and brownish, with jerky little movements and a cheeky air.' This character could turn out to be the murderer, but no one is going to 'detect' him straight away. We all have sympathy for sparrows.

Or consider: 'She was small and exquisite, with an expression of perpetual disdain on her porcelain-pale face.' This image is chilling: she could be imagined putting a lethal dose into a bedtime mug of hot milk. The reader will fasten on to her, because the introduction is angled unsympathetically. This sort of introduction to a character can be used as part of the general misdirection which the crime writer uses to tease the reader.

Readers go villain-spotting very early on. It is a cliché that the least likely character is the one who is 'It', and aware of this, crime writers have to be subtle in their introductions of their criminals. A useful device is to have another character – unpleasant, crotchety, tyrannical or vicious – upon whom the reader may latch as the villain.

Where red herrings are being used to cloak the identity of the murderer, it is recommended, when introducing them, to show only face value, and not investigate their personalities until suspicion begins to turn towards them.

The characters need to be fleshed out, given speech and actions which suit the type of persons you intend them to be. In the preparatory notes, you have given them a biography, an appearance and a temperament. You know their faults, as well as their virtues. Each of them has a specific part to play in the plot, and the writer has designed them for this.

It is possible to make mistakes, especially in early attempts at crime writing. These are nothing to worry about – the learning process is one of trial and error – but they are disconcerting, and are rooted in faulty planning.

Generally, the characters concerned are the vital ones of hero or villain. From the first, their roles are so sharply defined in the writer's mind that it is possible to neglect exploring them as people. It is only when one is halfway through the book – and developing these characters along logical lines – that it becomes clear that X is genuinely benevolent, and would never stick a knife into anyone, no matter what the provocation; or that Y is an utter swine underneath his/her delightful exterior. At the planning stage, characters are no more than outlines. It is only in the actual writing that the author gets to know the characters, to like or dislike them, and to find out if they are truly fitted to their roles. This can modify the author's perceptions, bringing dissatisfaction with a particular character, and demanding change.

Any sign of dissatisfaction is a warning signal, to be ignored at the writer's peril. One can be sure that the readers will pick up the fault.

Admittedly, this sort of thing is more likely to happen to a writer who works in a relatively unstructured way, but it is also a sad fact that, no matter how careful the initial planning, it can happen to anyone. It is due to the creative process, which is a mysterious thing taking place in the subconscious. All the necessary elements will be present in your plot, already hatched by the interior creative mind. The writer's job is to unlock the plot, and you may not get it right at the first go. Just as it is possible to begin the book from the wrong place, so can one tangle the roles of the characters before the creative process has begun.

This may seem to be a total catastrophe, but it does not have to be the end of the book. Trust the creative instinct and examine the other characters to see if one can take over the role. More often than not a suitable character is to hand. The book that emerges at the end will be all the better.

Hiding the clues

The hiding of clues is indicated in the synopsis. In the writing of the book, the task is to conceal each clue so that, with luck, the average reader will miss it, remembering only at the final explanation that the clue had been given.

The way to do it is to slip in the clue under the cover of some piece of action, which will divert the reader's attention, rather in the manner of a conjuror duping his audience. Example:

> As I passed the house, I could see Jane moving about the kitchen. On impulse, I walked up the path and knocked at the back door.
> 'Is that you, Ellen? Come on in.'
> 'No. It's me, Rita.'
> Jane flung open the door. She was crying. 'I saw someone pass the window. I thought it might be my

niece. I'm so glad you're here, Rita. I really don't know what to do.'

Attention is fixed upon Jane's trouble, but underneath there is a clue hidden: Jane mistook Rita for Ellen because both young women are the same size and shape, due to an unacknowledged blood relationship.

Clues can be slipped into general conversations, local gossip, arguments, while attention is held by some other topic. Or they can be shown openly, but because they are out of context, their importance escapes the other characters – and, hopefully, the readers, too. An example of this occurs in the worked example, where the finding of one of Simmonds's earrings in Lorna's flat, and the recognition that it belonged to her is open, but, set into a strained conversation with Mrs English and Brian, its importance is missed by Lorna.

Dialogue

The use of dialogue gives an edge over both reported speech and plain text. It is more interesting to read, more concise, and there is feedback from the other characters.

Speech patterns

Patterns of speech vary from person to person. The way of speaking is highly individual and indicative of certain traits of character. We all know people who are so anxious to air their own views that they snatch the words out of another's mouth, and people who chime in on the last few words of a sentence once they see where it is going. Others never finish a sentence and yet others ramble off on to their own pet subject no matter what everyone else is talking about. The variations are endless.

Dialogue is a dynamic way of writing, but is has to ring true. Listen to the dialogue in your own head. If possible, give the different characters their own quirks of speech. Imagine that this is not a novel but a radio play, where there is nothing but the voice to distinguish one character from another. Think of your characters in that situation and work out how you would deal with the problem. This will lead you to adjusting the pattern of speech to suit each character. This does not have to be anything outlandish: the generation gap is felt not only in age but in ways of speech, vocabulary and phraseology.

Accents

One obvious way of differentiating between characters is to give them regional accents. Check the biographical notes you have written on your characters to see where there may be differences of accent due to locality, education or class.

This may lead into the further problem of dialect, where, in addition to the regional accent, there are also grammatical differences. It is unwise to be tempted too far along this road. Dialect should be no more than hinted at, with only the odd bit put in to remind the reader of the origin of the character. Reading a passage written wholly in dialect is a trying experience.

Converting ordinary speech into dialogue

Creating dialogue out of speech is not as straightforward as one might imagine. The ordinary speech of many people consists of unco-ordinated or unfinished sentences, hesitations, catchwords and leaps about from one topic to another. This jumble has to be disciplined into something that sounds like ordinary speech, but conveys the conversation necessary to the scene.

There should be no hesitation over the use of slang, for all that it changes constantly and may be already old-fashioned by the time the book is published. Slang is in common use, and is evidence of a living language in course of development. Also, it is fun and colourful. Nevertheless, slang should be used with discretion, and care should be taken over more 'way out' expressions which might not be understood.

Swear words are a different matter. There are people

whose pattern of speech is such that every other word is an obscenity. This makes for difficult listening in the flesh and tiresome reading in a book. It may be a living pattern of speech, but the repetition of these words is boring.

How much of the swearing should be put into the dialogue is a matter of personal choice. In my view, it is better to use the offending words occasionally – a scatter of them over the lines of dialogue – rather than have the wearisome repetition.

The position is more difficult when there is a question-and-answer dialogue, and the unfortunate interrogator receives only one reply to all his questions.

Q: What were you doing at Joe's Caff?
A: Get f . . . d.
Q: Why did you go down the alley at the side?
A: Get f . . . d.

In real life, this sort of dialogue goes on until one or other gives up. In my view, a novel should not stick so close to reality, since nothing is being achieved by that interview – it adds up to an eminently skippable page. No amount of fidelity to realism can make up for a reader being given a chance to skip.

Conveying background information

Dialogue is one of the means of dealing with the background information concerning events which took place before the opening of the book. Material, which otherwise might have to be conveyed by flashback or prose explanations, can be given to the reader through conversations between characters. Read the following passage:

'Of course, he would, wouldn't he?' said the char, knowingly.
Her employer was surprised. 'He's done it before?'
'It was before you came here. Ten years back, easy. But there's still folks around who remember that woman. Tipped out into the snow, she was, bag and baggage.'

Descriptions of both people and places can be conveyed vividly through dialogue. For example:

> 'I went there, once,' said Kitty, morosely. 'In the rain. Streets and streets of grimy terrace houses with shiny wet slates, the pit with its big wheel standing idle, and nothing to do on a Sunday except go to chapel. Ghastly.'

Dialogue length

Dialogue has to be kept short. People usually speak in short bursts. If one member of a group holds the floor for any length of time, the others become restive, and this can also happen to readers. Any necessary long speech or explanation needs to be broken up in order to stimulate the reader's attention. This can be done by an interruption, or a quick change of focus to let the reader see the reactions of the characters who are listening.

Particular care should be taken in the final stage of the story, when all has to be explained. Sadly, explanations can be boring. If they are complicated, they may not be clearly understood if made in a large chunk of unbroken speech. Take time to make sure that the reader grasps fully the train of reasoning, line of thought, or narration of how the events come to a head.

Break up the dialogue with feedback from the listeners: questions, exclamations, tears, faints, denunciations. The effect is more lively and it ensures that the reader understands the dénouement of the story and will lay the book down satisfied, and sorry that it is finished.

One rule on the writing of dialogue should be borne in mind: always make sure that the reader knows exactly who is speaking any particular line, especially when it is a conversation between two characters; there is nothing more irritating than having to count the lines backward to determine the speaker.

Finishing the book

Writing the final word is a wonderful moment, the end of a long and arduous, but enjoyable journey. Remember to check the novel carefully, to make sure there are no inconsistencies, missing explanations, and all ends are neatly tied up.

Then put the typescript aside for a week or two. After that, reread it, preferably aloud. Be prepared for shocks. All sorts of things will jar upon you, and you will discover faults you had not noticed before, or things not expressed as well as might be. Now is the time to correct all that, not when you receive a printer's proof for checking – it's too late then.

9

BUSINESS MATTERS

Marketing the book

Every writer should aim at being published, appreciate that many difficulties lie in the way, and grit the teeth and get on with the job. Writers can increase their chances of acceptance by paying attention to presentation.

The book is written, but there is still a lot of work to be done on it. No matter how vigilant you are, faults will be found. Go through it carefully, correcting grammatical and typing errors.

You may decide that it needs further work in the way of polishing and improvements. You may have thought that you had done a really good job, but the truth is that there is always a better way of expressing yourself. Polishing starts as a few amendments, but these can reach such proportions that a complete rewrite will be necessary.

If a publisher suggests that you rewrite, do not argue. Get on with it. Our books are like precious children to us, but not to the world at large. Surgery may be necessary if the book is to be published.

It can happen that even a well-written book simply does not work in its original form. The underlying cause will lie, in all probability, in the construction of the plot, or the angle from which it is written. It may be necessary to change the theme, or to concentrate on another character. Every basic idea can furnish several themes. Try another. In any case, do not throw the book away in disgust. Put it on the back burner for a while before having another go at it. An interval of time frequently works wonders.

Preparing the typescript

It is of the utmost importance to submit a decent-looking script. A bad visual first impression on a publisher or reader puts the author at a disadvantage from the start.

Here are some tips to make sure that your novel is properly presented:

- It must be typed. If you write in longhand, or are a poor typist, send it out to be done. If you use a word processor, make sure that the printout is of high quality. Publishers' readers cannot be blamed for feeling irritated if the typescript is difficult to read.
- Use double-spacing, on standard A4 typewriter paper, with good margins, and the text on one side of the paper only. This gives space for the copy-editor to mark it up for the printer, and the typesetter must be able to read both the text and the marking-up.
- Number the pages. To differentiate between the pages of the typescript and the pages of the printed book, learn to call typescript pages 'folios', which is the publishers' name for them. This is important if, for any reason, an extra folio of typescript has to be included. In this case, give it the same number as the preceding folio with the letter 'a' after it. The following example shows exactly how to insert it into the typescript: Folio 15a has to be inserted. At the bottom of Folio 15, write at the foot 'Folio 15a follows'; at the foot of folio 15a, write 'Folio 16 follows'. If this is done, there is no danger that the inserted folio will be missed or lost.
- Do not submit a typescript covered in longhand corrections of your own. The folios should be retyped.
- Clip the folios of each chapter together with an ordinary slip-on paperclip. Do not staple the pages.
- Do not put the typescript into a fancy binder. Put it into a cardboard envelope folder.
- On the first folio put: the title: the approximate number of words: and your name and address. It is not necessary to count every word. Estimate the number by counting the words on four or five lines on a folio, and multiplying by the number of lines. Do this for a few folios, then

take an average. Multiply this by the total number of
folios, deducting for half-folios at the end of chapters.

- To protect the typescript, a stiffer piece of paper may
  be put at front and back.
- It is recommended that your name and address should
  also appear on the last folio.

Titles

The right title for the book may come to mind in the early
stages of planning, or it may not come at all, and the book
has to be given a temporary 'working title', with the final
title decided later between author, publisher's editor and
agent.

Finding the right title can be difficult. It needs to convey
something essential about the book; to be eye-catching; and
to alert the prospective reader to the type of book it is.

For a crime book, the prime need is for the title to suggest
murder, mayhem, suspense etc. What it must *not* do, is
allow the book be confused with, say, an historical novel,
For example, a tense courtroom drama could have for its
title *Sword of Justice*. This would be a mistake. The word
'sword' conjures up images of the Three Musketeers and
men prancing about in doublet and hose, waving rapiers.
With that sort of title, the book could fall foul of the wrong
readership and be missed by the readers for whose entertainment it was written.

It is almost impossible to find a title which has not been
used before. Accept this as a fact of literary life. All that
concerns the writer is that there should not be another book
currently in print with that title. If there is, another title will
have to be found. Do not be discouraged; the chances are
that the new title will be better than the first.

Submission

It is a waste of everyone's time if a novel is sent to the
wrong type of publisher. Check with the list in *The Writers'*

And Artists' Yearbook for publishing houses which handle crime fiction. Cross-check with the books on view in the public library and the bookshops.

How to submit a typescript

- Send a preliminary letter to the selected publisher, asking if they will look at it. It is helpful to include a synopsis and the first two chapters. If the publisher thinks it might fit into his list, he will ask you to send the complete typescript.
- Pack the typescript safely, preferably in a padded bag. Enclose the return postage. There is no point in sending it by registered post, although recorded delivery will enable you to check that the parcel arrived.
- Always keep a copy for yourself, updated with any last-minute changes.
- Be patient. Wait at least two months before making any sort of inquiry – and then do it in the form of a *very tactful* letter.
- When submitting to another publisher after one or more rejections, check the typescript for marks, dog-eared corners, etc. The new publisher will not be favourably impressed by the sight of a tired and tatty typescript which looks as if it has been everywhere. Replace the first and the last few folios with clean new ones.
- Never despair and be tempted into vanity publishing. If the book is good enough, it will eventually find a publisher. Persevere.

Agents

The job of an agent is to be a channel through which writers sell their work. There is no regulation which lays down that marketing a book has to be done this way, but working through an agent brings certain advantages. They know where to offer a book, and which publisher is most likely to take it, and they are in contact with agents abroad, so foreign sales are a possibility.

In practice, the relationship with one's agent is closer than the marketing mechanism would suggest. Founded upon mutual self-interest, with luck it will develop into one of mutual loyalty. Agents give advice. It pays to take notice of it; it is difficult for a writer to keep abreast of what is happening in the publishing houses, and the agent's finger is on the pulse. The knowledge that a good agent is working for you and is on your side is a great comfort, for writing is a lonely business.

These days it is difficult for a beginner to find an agent. This does not mean that it is futile to try. *The Writers' and Artists' Yearbook* contains a list of agents. Each entry indicates the type of work that is handled.

How to approach an agent

Write a preliminary letter, enclosing a synopsis of the book and the first two chapters. Always enclose return postage. An agent, once he or she finds a promising new writer, will go to a lot of trouble to encourage them. This is an investment in the future of that writer, since most agents are paid only when they take their well-earned commission on the sale of the book.

A word of warning: do not expect an agent to teach you how to write or to provide you with a long criticism – or any at all – of a work they consider unsuitable.

Agreements

On acceptance of a book by a publisher, a royalty agreement is prepared. Royalties are the percentage paid to the author on all copies sold. It is customary for an 'advance' on these royalties to be paid on signature of the agreement.

If you are dealing directly with the publisher, you should read all the clauses of the agreement carefully before signature. In case of doubt, ask a literary agent to look at it, or approach the Society of Authors. There is a detailed article on the subject of publishing practice in *The Writers' and Artists' Yearbook*.

Proof-reading

In the course of publication of the book, the writer will receive proofs for checking. This is a wearisome and difficult job. As the author, you will be so familiar with the text that you will probably find it very difficult to see small errors.

It is recommended that, in addition to working on the proofs yourself, you should enlist the help of a friend.

With modern methods of typesetting, corrections to proofs are very expensive and must be limited to the printers' own errors. If you insist on making alterations to the text at this late stage, you may find yourself presented with the bill for them.

In correcting proofs, printers' marks have to be used. A table of these marks and instructions on their use is to be found in *The Writers' and Artists' Yearbook*.

Blurbs

Some publishers require their authors to write the blurb to go on the inside of the dust jacket. The aim of this is to tempt the reader to read the book.

Writing a blurb is not an easy task. Enough has to be said to intrigue the reader, but not so much that the whole plot is given away. A limit is set on the amount of words required for the blurb, which is a help.

Giving the thing the necessary force and appeal is really an advertising man's job. Writers are obliged to do it. My own view is that it is easier to write the book.

Copyright

Copyright protection applies to original works, which, in law, means that it is the product of skill and labour on the part of the author. It lasts for fifty years after the end of the calendar year in which the author dies.

There is no copyright on ideas. Copyright protects the

form – that is, the book – in which the idea is worked out, but not the idea itself.

This is important because it is a strange fact that ideas seem to go in fashions, and the same one will strike a number of writers, widely scattered, at more or less the same time. This mystery leads to a lot of trouble, with people accusing others of stealing their ideas.

All too frequently, ideas are offered to writers by people who can only be described as authors' pests. Their offers do not arise out of friendship, but out of hopes of gain from an author who uses their idea, does all the work, and gives them at least half the proceeds. My invariable response is to congratulate these people on a good idea, and suggest that they write it themselves.

An idea, once encountered in another book, can be stored away in the memory and surface perhaps years later, when the writer has forgotten whence it came. There is no guilt attached to this, and it is unlikely that the development of the idea will result in an identical book; however, if the development happens by the direst of ill fortune to come out close to the original, someone is sure to say: 'Oh, I remember that story, from such-and-such.'

Even though the writer is innocent of any form of plagiarism that is a disaster. If one person can 'recognise' the work, so can others. The worst charge to be made against an author is that of plagiarism.

Plagiarism is an infringement of copyright, because the *form* of the work has been taken. Regrettably, on occasions, it does happen.

Public Lending Right

The battle for the right to royalties on borrowings from public libraries was long and hard fought. The system applies only to public library loans over the counter. Loans are counted from a 'sample' of thirty public libraries, from regions scattered all over the UK. This sample is changed every two or three years.

Authors have to register their books with the Registrar of Public Lending Right, and it is important to do this for each book as it is published. Advance registration is not permitted.

Funding is from central government. Payment per loan is very small – a fraction of a penny – but it is amazing how it can add up.

The writer's life

People write because they want to; it is an inner compulsion. Crime writers write to entertain, to give a little relaxation in a world of stress.

It is very hard work.

The writer has to face long hours of physical, as well as mental, labour. There are times when nothing will go right; when words squeezed past 'writer's block' are lifeless; when the clamour of the world sets up intense frustrations in the writer.

Disappointment has to be faced when no one wants your work and rejection slips pile up.

It is all part of the writer's lot. You have to believe in yourself and what you are doing. Acquire all possible technical skill – even the greatest talent needs to learn the disciplines of the craft. Be patient and work hard. There is always room for another good writer.

APPENDIX I – HOW TO KILL YOUR VICTIM

The investigation of crime is a highly professional and scientific procedure. The technology is complicated, but the concern of the writer is more with the results than with the nature of the tests: you need to know what your detective may expect from the pathologists and the forensic laboratories.

Choose your weapon

Blunt instruments

Almost any object, from a walking stick or a brick in a sock to an electric iron or a hammer, can be a blunt instrument. All the term implies is that the weapon does not have a sharp stabbing point or a cutting edge.

The problem from the murderer's point of view is that the blunt instrument may not kill at the first blow. Further blows can be extremely messy, even if the victim is unconscious.

The detective will find plenty of traces at the scene of the crime, on the weapon itself, and on the clothing of the perpetrator. Within the wounds, there are likely to be traces of anything with which the weapon has been in contact – for example, traces of grease of a piece of garage equipment. The shape and depth of the wounds will indicate the type of instrument used.

Knives and axes

The nature of the wound indicates the type of weapon. An incised wound, made with a razor or scalpel, is longer than it is deep or wide. A stab is greater in depth than in length or breadth.

Killing by stabbing is not difficult once the skin is penetrated. The knife is not, necessarily, a long one: the elasticity of the skin will permit considerable penetration by a small blade. The bleeding may be almost entirely internal.

Sometimes stab wounds produce strange results. Death from a fatal blow may not ensue immediately; victims have been known to walk away from the scene of the crime before collapsing.

Slashes and axe attacks generally produce a good deal of external bleeding.

If the victim gets a chance to fight back, there will be defence wounds on hands and arms.

Poison

Poison obtained from wild plants such as foxgloves, fungi, deadly nightshade, and hemlock is the classic method of murder down through the centuries. Until modern times, the crime went virtually undetected.

The most famous murder trials of the nineteenth century featured cases of arsenical poisoning, and there have been notable instances in modern times. Arsenic is easily detectable, and the traces remain in the corpse for a long time.

Another old favourite is cyanide, once used for rat poison and insecticide, now strictly controlled but used in industrial processes and agriculture. Cyanide comes in many forms, the best known being prussic acid and hydrogen cyanide gas. The most accessible are the alkaline cyanides, especially potassium cyanide.

Strychnine is the third 'Victorian' poison. It was, and still is, used in medical preparations as well as in animal poisons. It has a very bitter taste, and the symptoms are easily recognised.

A modern poison is paraquat, used to suppress weeds. There is no known antidote.

With the expanding use of drugs, both medical and illegal, the opportunities for unsuspected crime have increased. Suicides overdose on barbiturates. The problem for a murderer would be that of persuading the intended victim to take them. Crushing them up and adding the powder to food or drink would be unlikely to work, since the taste would be overpoweringly horrible even when disguised with sugar.

With all poisons, the question of dosage arises. People have differing levels of tolerance to poison. A doctor or pharmacist would know how much to give, while a layman would be inclined to overdose.

Firearms

The general public has only limited access to rifles and pistols. The criminal fraternity has its own suppliers of illegal shooters. These are not 'registered' weapons, and are likely to be broken up once they have been fired. Shotguns come into a different category. They are available everywhere, and certificates for the holding of them are routine; rural areas are full of them. Criminals shorten the barrels and the stock to turn a shotgun into an overgrown handgun. The result is a fearsome weapon, useful as a menace, but not accurate except at close range, when it will inflict a very nasty wound.

All weapons except shotguns have parallel grooves carved in spirals on the inside of the barrel to stabilise the bullet and keep it on its trajectory. Size goes according to the internal diameter of the barrel. Shotguns use cartridges which contain pellets to form a spread when fired. Shotguns are ten-, twelve- or sixteen-bore, an archaic classification based on the number of solid lead roundshot to the pound.

Firearms leave marks, individual to each weapon, such as rifling on a bullet or marks of the firing-pin on the cartridge case, for the forensic scientist to find. Automatic pistols will also leave marks from the ejector, magazine, bolt-face, chamber-wall and extractor.

Different types of firearms have different characteristics:

- Rifles – accuracy to about 2000 yards using high-velocity bullets; military rifles are mostly automatic and light-

140

weight. An example is the AR–15 Armalite, firing 800 rounds per minute of 5.66mm ammo, magazine holding 30 rounds; snipers use heavier rifles with more sophisticated sights, including infra-red and laser. These are bolt-action, hand loaded, with extra-long barrels.

- Pistols – revolvers hold rounds (usually six) or cartridges, and are very reliable. Examples are: calibres .22, .38 (standard US police issue), .357 (magnum, also used by police), .44. Automatics have a complicated mechanism which has a tendency to jam; magazines hold up to thirteen rounds and are fired by single pull on trigger. An example is the Walther 7.65 mm.
- Machine-guns – all automatic, professional military weapons, are used by terrorists, but rarely by ordinary criminals. An example is Ingram M–10, with a fire-rate about 1,200 per minute and a magazine holding 32 rounds.
- Shotguns – weapons with a short range of up to 80 yards, designed for shooting of game in motion. They are mostly double-barrelled; the single-barrel semi-automatic pump action is not widely used. Capable of killing a man at close-range.

Hanging

In real life, hangings are usually suicide or accident. There have been cases where a 'hanging' has been staged to cover up a murder, but the truth is always revealed when the rope is removed from the neck, genuine hanging leaving a deep bruise on the flesh at the point of pressure. Anything put round the neck after death would not normally show much of a mark. Death in hanging attempts is frequently due to cardiac arrest.

Asphyxiation

Asphyxiation occurs when the air supply to the blood is cut off, starving the tissues of oxygen. This is done in a number of ways:

- Suffocation – the supply of oxygen in the air is dangerously reduced or cut off by the presence of smoke, dense dust, smog, or unbreathable gases.
- Smothering – the external blockage of the nose and mouth. A pillow placed over the face of a child or old person will kill, but this is less likely to succeed in the case of an adult. A plastic bag placed over the head will kill very quickly.
- Choking – due to an object wedged in the windpipe, or a gag rammed into the mouth, causing an accumulation of saliva and mucus if left too long in place. Death occurs even though the nostrils are free.
- Manual strangulation – a frontal attack, causing fracture of the larynx and hyoid bones. A right-handed assailant will leave a thumb bruise on the right side of the victim's neck, and finger bruises on the left.
- Strangulation by ligature – an attack from the rear, using almost anything as a ligature, and less likely to fracture the bones of larynx and hyoid. The ridges of the ligature will show up as curves on the neck, giving no true indication of its width.

Most strangulations contain an element of cardiac arrest, as pressure on the carotid arteries cuts off the supply of blood to the brain. A sudden grabbing of the neck may produce the same effect. Traumatic asphyxiation comes from restriction of the breathing movements of the chest. The only known case of it as a murder method is that of the body-snatchers, Burke and Hare, who are supposed to have killed their victims by sitting on their chests.

Drowning

The victim dies of asphyxiation, but not with lack of oxygen as the main cause; it is the result of the fluid and chemical disturbances which take place in the blood that kills. This can occur rapidly.

Drowning in fresh water is quick – a matter of about four minutes. As soon as someone falls – or is pushed – into a lake or river, the immediate reaction is struggling and panic, and water is taken into the lungs, and into contact with the breathing membrane through which, to support life, air normally passes. The water passes through the membrane into the blood. Fresh water has not the same osmotic pressure as the blood; it increases the volume of the blood rapidly and dilutes it, upsetting the biochemical balance of the body. Death is inevitable.

Drowning in sea water gives the victim a better chance of survival if they are fished out. Salt water has the same osmotic pressure as the blood, so no massive fluid transfer takes place, although the level of sodium chloride (salt) rises. Death does not usually take place in under eight minutes, and may be up to twenty minutes.

The temperature of the water is important in drowning. Reflex cardiac arrest can take place on falling into water, especially if it is cold. Equally, a sudden douche of cold water against the back of the nose or throat can cause instant unconsciousness and death if the victim is not resuscitated quickly enough.

Murder victims are often disposed of by throwing the body into water. By natural processes, an immersed body will rise, sooner or later. Weighting down can prevent this, or merely serve to delay discovery, and so present the pathologist with a most unpleasant corpse. If decomposition is far advanced, it may prove impossible to determine the cause of death. Identification also may present serious problems.

Distinguishing between a body which has drowned and one which was dead when it entered the water is not so difficult. The signs of drowning are: fine froth in the air passages and lungs; debris in the air passages; cadaveric spasm of the fingers, retaining hold of underwaters weeds clutched at in the panic of drowning; the presence of microscopic water algae (diatoms) pumped round by the heart into the organs of the body in the last moments of life. A dead body dropped into water will have water in the lungs, and diatoms there, too: but the diatoms will be nowhere else.

Other methods

It has always been possible to arrange lethal traps such as accidents; fires; electrocutions in the bathrooom; tripwires; fixed motor cars; quick pushes over a cliff or down a flight of stairs. All leave traces for investigators to find. This is also true of specialised methods of killing, such as the use of karate chops or medical expertise.

Murder is best kept simple.

APPENDIX II – HOW THE BRITISH POLICE OPERATE

Unless you have chosen a closed setting, such as an island with no communication with the mainland, or a house cut off by snowdrifts, sooner or later, you will have to sketch in some details of the officials who uphold law and order. Police investigations will impinge upon the activities of other characters, even if your detective is an amateur. You need to know how the police work.

The system

In police terms, the United Kingdom is divided into Regions each made up of a county or a group of counties, depending upon the density of the population, which reflects in the crime rate. Within the Region, each county has its own police force, divided into Divisions and then into Sub-Divisions, each centred on one of the towns. The Metropolitan Police District (MPD), Headquarters at Scotland Yard, is divided into eight areas, and combines with the City of London Police to form a separate Region.

Command structures.

London

Metropolitan Police District
The Commissioner
Assistant Commissioners
Deputy Assistant Commissioners
(1 to each area)
Commanders
(2 to each area)

The City of London Police is commanded by a Commissioner. Subordinate ranks of both the MPD and the City of London Police are the same for the rest of the country – Chief Superintendent, Superintendent, Chief Inspector, Inspector, Sergeant and Constable.

Regions (outside London)

Policing is carried out by the police forces of the various counties to form the Region. Overall command is from Regional Headquarters.

Regional Headquarters
Chief Constable
Deputy Chief Constable
Assistant Chief Constables
Chief Superintendents i/c HQ Departments
Traffic & Communications
Administration
Personnel & Training
Operations (HQ Control Room)
CID (DCS i/c, Deputy and Scenes-of-Crime specialists.
No operational detectives. DCS or Deputy takes charge
of all major crime investigations in Region)

Each county force is divided into territorial Divisions.

Divisional Headquarters
Chief Superintendent
Superintendent
(Deputy)
Superintendents or Chief Inspectors
i/c
Administration
Uniformed Police
CID (Crime Squad, Incident Room)

Territorial Divisions have Sub-Divisions, and, at the bottom of the scale, Section Stations (in very small towns)

Sub-Division
Superintendent, Chief Inspector
or Inspector
i/c
Administration
Uniformed Police
CID (Inspector i/c)
Section Stations
Sergeant
Detective Sergeant or Constables
Uniformed Constables

Civilian staff

Civilians are employed for many secretarial posts. There is a Civilian Establishment Officer at Regional Headquarters, also a Welfare Officer, and a Press Officer. Increasingly, civilian experts are employed in scenes-of-crime investigations.

Regional Serious Crime Squads

Certain Regions have established Serious Crime Squads. These are not to take over the work of the CID; their function is mainly the collection of intelligence and investigation of major criminals, including those dealing in drugs. The advantage of having such a squad is that it can operate all over the Region without running into the difficulties which may be encountered when the officers of one force need to cross into the territory of another force. Regional Crime Squads are staffed by detectives on detachment from all the forces which comprise the Region. They are commanded by detective chief superintendents known as Regional Coordinators.

Other special squads

Fraud, rape, bombs, terrorism, robbery, drugs, vice, art thefts and other specialist crimes are dealt with by squads of detectives with particular skills.

Note: If you are intending to write a police procedural novel, you will have to go into the nature of policing, its structures and procedures, training, career opportunities, and the way a shift in the working day operates. The brief account above is intended only to make sure that writers give their police investigators the appropriate rank for the senior investigating officers of serious crimes, and that their position in the hierarchy is clear.

The scene of the crime

Most writers like to leave the finding of the corpse at the point where someone is screaming their head off, but it is as well to know what happens next.

On discovery of a dead body, someone has to fetch the nearest police constable. This man then sends for his sergeant. Both these officers will be from the uniformed branch. The sergeant will inform CID at Sub-Division. If he sees anything suspicious about the corpse, he asks for the DCI or the DI. The area is cordoned off, with a passageway marked off so that as little as possible of the site is trampled. A log of all persons visiting the scene is opened.

The DI from Sub-Division visits the scene, and immediately informs CID at Regional HQ. The duty Detective Superintendent is despatched to the scene, no matter what time of day or night.

Before anything can be done, the Police Surgeon (a local doctor appointed to this duty) has to pronounce the victim dead.

The Scene-of-Crime Officer arrives. This person is likely to be a civilian Scientific Officer. His job is to preserve the scene for the investigating officers.

The pathologist on duty is informed. He will probably be a university professor, and may have to travel a considerable distance to the mortuary (usually in a hospital) where he will carry out the post-mortem examination. This is done as soon as possible.

The Detective Superintendent inspects the body, notifies Divisional HQ, and requests the attendance of the forensic team.

Photographs and video recordings are taken. The Coroner is informed and gives permission for the body to be removed to the mortuary.

CID investigation

As soon as a major crime is reported and the forensic team sent, the Incident Room is opened up. This is a purpose-built room at Divisional HQ, complete with telephones, computers, typewriters, filing cabinets and so on, and a trained staff ready to move in at any time. The computers are linked to the HOMES (Home Office Major Enquiry System) central computer, so that any correlation may be pinpointed quickly. At the scene of the crime a Forward Post is set up, either at the nearest police station or in a caravan.

The first twenty-four hours of an investigation are very busy. Basic inquiries are made immediately, and everything is logged and put on to computers. The uniformed branch provide labour for intensive searches of the area surrounding the scene of the crime, and house-to-house inquiries. This is done under the command of the DI or Detective Sergeant. Investigating officers from all over the region are drafted in to take charge of these teams.

The police have the right to question anyone whom they think may have relevant information, but no one is compelled to answer except in a court witness box. If suspicion points to a particular person, they are invited to accompany the investigating officer to a police station to 'help the police with their inquiries'. The suspect has to consent to this. Under Judges' Rule, the suspect has to be cautioned. The exact words are: 'You are not obliged to say anything unless you wish to do so, but what you say may be put in writing and given in evidence.' A second caution is given once a suspect is charged. This is the same as the first caution, but must be preceded by the question: 'Do you wish to say anything?'

The post-mortem examination (autopsy)

This has to be carried out as soon as possible; corpses are not left waiting overnight. As soon as the pathologist arrives, the work is begun. Mortuary facilities are usually provided by the local hospital if there is no separate facility. The pathologist is appointed by the Home Office, and is likely to be a university professor.

Officers attending include: the Senior Investigating Officer; the Scene-of-Crime Officer; the Coroner's Officer (usually a constable); the police photographer and video recorder operator.

The main purpose of the post-mortem is to establish the cause of death. It is in the general interest that the post-mortem should be done as carefully as possible, and everything recorded. If the murderer is caught and brought to trial, the defence will have the right to demand a second post-mortem, with embarrassing results of anything is proved to have been missed.

Over recent years the video recorder has come into use at the scene of the crime and also at the post-mortem, backing up notes taken by hand and dictated on to tape, as well as still photographs. The playing back of a video gives much more information than notes and stills.

The first stage is 'naked-eye observations'. The pathologist describes the body as he finds it, detailing every abnormal sign before he opens it up. Then the body is fingerprinted, and samples of the hair, from behind nails, from vagina and anus, blood, urine, stomach contents, lungs, are taken which will be analysed in about twenty-four hours. After this, incisions are made and organs removed. Sections are cut of bruises, abrasions, lung tissue; wounds are examined and measured, then dissected.

Estimating the time of death is very difficult, since body type, physical condition before death, as well as outside climatic conditions produce endless variations. Old theories of the rate of cooling are no longer accepted. Nor is rigor mortis a good index of the time of death. It can commence as early as two hours after death and pass off after twenty-four hours, but it can be fully developed as late as fifty hours after death. Decomposition in the British climate begins at about thirty-six hours. Cadaveric rigidity happens at the moment of death, and often leaves a hand clutching something. This cannot be faked. An object put into a hand stiffening in the normal process of rigor mortis will not be clutched in the same way.

With all these variants, no pathologist can commit himself to a definite time of death. All he will do is estimate a wide period of time within which the death took place. The contents of the stomach can narrow this down if it is known when the last meal was eaten.

The pathologist may be asked to provide clues as to the identity of the deceased. Much depends on the condition of the body. If flesh is still present, it is possible to obtain fingerprints, even when the corpse has been immersed in water. Teeth, scars and tattoos, blood type, occupational marks such as callouses on hands due to tools or musical instruments, all help to narrow down the field of investigation. If the remains are skeletal, the bones can furnish evidence of sex, stature, age, and race; malformations from past injuries or disease; presence of marks indicating crimes; marks of burning or other efforts to destroy the body. What cannot be proved, if all soft tissue has gone, is death due to poisoning or asphyxia. The very fact of concealment of a body suggests that the discovery and identification of the remains may well lead to the apprehension of a murderer. The classic illustration of this is the Buck Ruxton case of 1935, where the bodies of the two victims were cut up into no less than seventy small pieces and scattered. Two left feet proved to be the undoing of the murderous Dr Ruxton.

The use of dental records to identify badly damaged corpses, particularly as a result of a fire or long immersion in water, brings the dentist on to the scene. Bite marks can also be matched to the teeth which made them. Marks and stains on teeth can suggest the type of work done by the deceased – wind musicians, and people who in the course of their work habitually hold nails or needles between their teeth, develop dental marks; those working with metals such as lead and copper acquire chemical deposits on their teeth; so do smokers, but cigarettes and pipes leave stains in different places.

The post-mortem can give indications of what has happened to the body after death. If it has been dragged, there will be abrasions; if it has been moved shortly after death, post-mortem staining will show where the blood has drained down in the body in its initial position after death. But if the body is moved after, say, half an hour, the still-liquid blood will drain into the new position, giving two lots of staining.

Gunshot wounds are complicated. Great care has to be taken by the pathologist in differentiating between entry and exit wounds before any sections are cut. There has been a lot of argument over this in the case of the assassination of President Kennedy. Once inside the body, a bullet can travel in odd fashions. If it is still inside, x-rays may have to be taken to find it.

After the post-mortem examination, the cadaver is sewn up again and left neat and tidy in case a second examination is ordered. Then it is refrigerated until the coroner authorises its disposal.

The forensic laboratory

These are Home Office establishments – currently there are seven of them – scattered around the country. Their work is not confined to a particular locality. Each laboratory has its own speciality and receives material from all police regions.

The forensic laboratory takes up where the post-mortem examination leaves off, and processes the samples taken. It analyses stains; hairs; poison traces in body tissue, paints and varnishes; dust and dirt and scrapings from scenes of crime; examines fire residues where arson is suspected; compares glass fragments, tracks and impressions from vehicles and human feet, pollen grains, seeds and leaves; compares clothing from victims and suspects, and rifle marks from firearms. The scientific truth is that everything picks up something from its environment, and no two environments are exactly the same.

The work falls into three main categories: biology, which deals with murder, wounding and rape, analysing swabs, bloodstains, hairs and fibres; toxicology, concerned with poisons and drug abuse; chemistry, devoted to the analysis of samples of material things – paint flakes, metals, glass – and fires. The work overlaps when, for instance, the contents of a stomach are analysed; then all three departments may be involved. It is a world of high technology, with all results fed into computers.

University laboratories contribute much research, for example, on DNA 'fingerprinting', based on body fluids, which is used in identifying sex offenders; the superimposition of photographs upon skulls to assist in identification of bodies; the rebuilding of whole heads on the top of skulls, which produces a most lifelike impression, far superior to any artist's reconstruction of what an unidentified skeleton may have looked like in life. 'Offender profiling' is a new technique being developed by Professor David Canter, working from the nature of a repeated offence in a certain area, establishing a pattern from locations, and using the principles of environmental psychology to produce a 'profile' of the offender.

University dental schools house the few experts in forensic odontology, an important sphere in which Western Europe lags behind Russia.

Forensic science has come a long way in the past hundred years. In the 1880s Bertillon was perfecting his method of anthropometry to identify habitual criminals, and Herschel in India and Faulds in Japan experimented with fingerprints. In 1892 Galton published the first book on fingerprinting, which was developed by Henry into the Galton-Henry system, used in many countries. Now we have the National Identification Bureau (successor to the CRO) and Regional

Criminal Intelligence Offices. Faced with comparison microscopes, gas chromatography, laser microspectral analysers and the rest of the advanced scientific instruments of the forensic laboratory, it seems unbelievable that it was only in 1900 that a test was devised for distinguishing between human and animal blood.

APPENDIX III – THE LEGAL SYSTEM IN ENGLAND AND WALES

With the exception of those who set their novels inside law courts, the writer normally does not need to know much about what happens once the guilty party has been apprehended by the police. However, many stories start off with the wrong person in custody, and in the course of the novel it is necessary to know what is likely to be happening to them. The purpose of this section is to give a rundown of the parts of the legal process with which the characters may be concerned.

The inquest

The office of Coroner is one of great antiquity. For at least the last eight hundred years, these Crown Officers have concerned themselves in the matter of sudden death.

The body is in the Coroner's charge: his permission is required for moving it from the place of death, for the autopsy and for its disposal.

The inquest has to be opened as quickly as possible, at the most, two days after the discovery of the body. At this stage, identification evidence only is taken. If this is not yet possible, the body has to be kept under refrigeration until the identity is established.

The Coroner can release the body for disposal once it has been identified, but in a murder case the body can only be buried. It may be required to be exhumed later. Cremation is not permitted, for obvious reasons.

Since the Criminal Law Act of 1978, no one can be

charged with murder by the jury at an inquest. From a novelist's point of view, this is rather a pity; juicy scenes are now denied to us. The practical reasons behind this reform are that such a charge could seriously hamper the police investigation, and the person named would have to be sent for trial, whether or not there was sufficient evidence against them.

Under the present system, once evidence of identification has been taken, the Coroner adjourns the inquest. Once someone is charged with the crime, under normal police procedures, the inquest is adjourned until after the trial.

Arrest and remand

The Police and Criminal Evidence Act 1984 has changed the rights of the citizen and the powers of the police.

Rights of the citizen

1. A person who attends voluntarily at a police station can leave at will. If there are grounds to suspect some offence, the volunteer must be cautioned, and is then classed as a 'suspect'.
2. Any person has a common-law right to remain silent.
3. No one can be kept in police detention for more than twenty-four hours without being charged unless he/she is arrested for a Serious Arrestable Offence (SAO) when other considerations apply.
4. A suspect not under arrest, or a person arrested and held in custody, has an absolute right to legal advice in private at any time.
5. A suspect has a right to have one person notified of the fact of his arrest and place of detention.

NB. Point no. 4 is an innovation. It is the first time that this statutory right has been granted, and there is a chance that it could be abused by persons facing charges for serious offences. (See below, under 'Powers of the police'.)

APPENDIX III

Powers of the police

1. Detention without charge is permitted for such time as necessary for the custody officer to decide if there is enough evidence to charge the suspect; or else if his detention is necessary to secure or preserve evidence, or obtain such evidence by questioning him.
2. A person arrested for an SAO may be kept in detention for more than twenty-four hours.
3. Detention up to thirty-six hours may be authorised by a police superintendent.
4. Detention beyond thirty-six hours must be authorised by a court.
5. Authorisation must be given in stages up to a maximum of ninety-six hours.
6. The police have the right to question anyone from whom information may be obtained relevant to an offence under investigation.
7. The police have power to delay any access to a solicitor for up to thirty-six hours, as decided by a superintendent, where an SAO is involved and there are reasonable grounds for believing that access to a solicitor would lead to interference with evidence, injury to other persons, or will lead to the alerting of other persons suspected but not yet arrested, or will hinder the recovery of property taken as a result of the offence.

Remand

A remand in custody cannot be for longer than eight days. If the defendant is to be kept in police cells, the maximum period is three days.

Magistrates have no power to try a person charged with any offence triable only at the Crown Court. Such a person will be remanded to appear before the Crown Court, and no date is fixed for the expiry of the remand. The accused is remanded to a date which will be notified to him by the appropriate officer of the Crown Court.

Prosecution

The decision whether or not to prosecute rests with the Department of the Director of Public Prosecutions (in England and Wales). The police have made an arrest, and, possibly, already charged the suspect, but it is the Area Crown Prosecutor who will make the decision from the file which the police present to him. This will contain all the statements of witnesses and all other relevant evidence.

The Crown Prosecutor's staff will examine this material for evidence admissible in law and on which there is a reasonable chance of obtaining a conviction. If there is, committal proceedings will be taken against the accused. The Crown Prosecutor must send copies of all statements to the defence, at that time, and must also send any which come in later.

The defence is not bound by any such rule, and may, at the trial, give the Crown a nasty surprise. The exception to this relates to alibis. If the defendant is proposing to claim that he was elsewhere (the exact meaning of the word 'alibi') the Crown has to be notified so that the police can interview witnesses and check the alibi. If it stands up, the charges may be dropped at this stage.

A point to note: if the charges are dropped at the committal stage, the defendant has not been *tried*. Therefore, if further evidence comes to light to substantiate the original charge, there is no impediment – no plea of double jeopardy – to prevent the person from being re-arrested.

The trial will be held in the Crown Court. The prisoner has the right to object to three jurors without having to give a reason. If the defence wishes to object to more, reasons must be given. The old right of peremptory challenge to the jury has been abolished since January 1989.

The prosecution opens the case. Witnesses are called, and cross-examined by both sides; the prosecutor makes his final speech and the defence lawyer has the last say; the judge sums up, and directs the jury on points of law.

The jury retire. If they cannot reach a unanimous verdict after at least two hours, they are permitted to reach a majority verdict, or, after a long period, to return to the court unable to agree. At that point, either the trial starts all over again with a fresh jury or the DPP decides to drop the charges, and a 'not guilty' verdict is pronounced.

In crime writing, the great courtroom battle is essentially an American phenomenon. Under the English system of justice, barristers are not permitted to 'do a Perry Mason'. They will slice up hostile witnesses, but there is not the freedom of action to make a prolonged account of the proceedings exciting enough to hold a reader's attention. Where a trial is essential to the plot, it is better to treat it from the viewpoint of the people involved, moving the focus from one to another.

Note: Scotland has its own legal system, due to the introduction of Roman law in the sixteenth century. While the laws are broadly the same as for the rest of the United Kingdom, the administration differs. The Law Officers bear different titles: for example, the Coroner's work is done by the Procurator Fiscal. Scottish juries have the right to return a verdict of 'not proven' when they can neither condemn nor acquit.